BIRDER'S GUIDE

TO

SOUTHWESTERN MANITOBA

by

Calvin W. Cuthbert

Jean I. Horton

Mamie W. McCowan

Barbara G. Robinson

Norman G. Short

Published by the authors
in co-operation with
Brandon Natural History Society
I.S.B.N. 0-920436-37-4

DEDICATION

This book is dedicated to our families in appreciation of their encouragement, patience and support.

PREFACE

Within recent years there has been increased interest as to where to find those most "sought after" birds in southwestern Manitoba. At the initiation of Cal Cuthbert and under his leadership, this birder's guide has been prepared by a team of birders of Brandon Natural History Society. Its purpose is to give information on the best seasonal birding spots and on the overall distribution and abundance of birds to be seen in the region. As knowledge of birds in the southwestern region of Manitoba increases, revisions of this book are anticipated.

Good birding!

ACKNOWLEDGEMENTS

Front cover - Mountain Bluebird, by Audrah Caughell

Back cover - Gray Partridge, by Stan Good

Sketches - Cal Cuthbert

Maps - Doug Glucki

Bar Graphs - Norman Short

Manuscript - Joan Rollheiser

The authors would like to thank the many people who contributed information, gave financial support, and assisted in other ways towards the preparation and publication of this guide.

Special thanks are due to Ken De Smet for reviewing the bar graphs; Rudolf Koes for additional records; Dr. Richard Rounds, Director of the Rural Development Institute, Brandon University, for advice on printing, and Brandon Natural History Society for support and encouragement from the inception of the project.

Dr. Richard W. Knapton's publication "Birds of the Gainsborough-Lyleton Region (Saskatchewan and Manitoba)" has been a useful reference.

CONTENTS

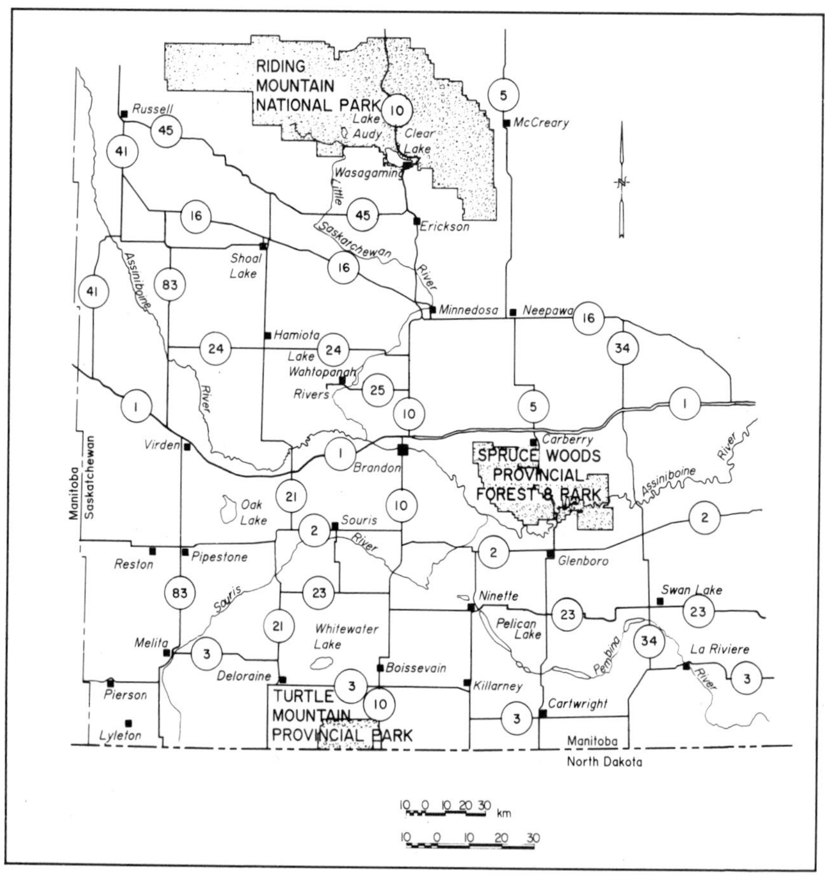

M1 SOUTHWESTERN MANITOBA

INTRODUCTION

The region

The region covered by this guide is outlined on M1 (page 2). Brandon, Manitoba's second largest city with a population of approximately 40,000, is situated near the centre of the guide area.

While agriculture has largely altered the landscape of southwestern Manitoba from its original, predominantly grassland state, a wide variety of habitats remains. From pockets of native mixed-grass prairie in the southwest corner to the boreal forest in Riding Mountain National Park an impressive seasonal diversity of birds may be found. The river systems, particularly the Assiniboine, Souris and Little Saskatchewan Rivers with their valleys and river-bottom woodlands, and the Pembina River with its series of narrow lakes, provide relief from the surrounding, gently rolling terrain. The river valleys offer some of the best remaining natural habitat and locations for seeing birds. The extreme southwest with its open expanses of mixed-grass prairie provides breeding habitat for western species rare elsewhere in the province.

Created by glaciation, wetlands in the form of potholes and sloughs occur in a large area extending from the Tri-Lakes area north and west towards Riding Mountain National Park. Unfortunately extensive draining of these small but important water bodies has resulted in restricted breeding habitat for many marshland birds including waterfowl.

Notable hills in the region include the Brandon Hills, Carberry Sand Hills (Spruce Woods area), Tiger Hills, Turtle Mountain, Oak Lake Sand Hills and Riding Mountain National Park. The largest, most diverse and most rugged of these is Riding Mountain. The Manitoba escarpment runs in a northwest to southeast line from north of Riding Mountain to the United States border. This escarpment is particularly evident along the east side of Riding Mountain and, with a drop of some 450 metres, is the most impressive topographical feature in the region.

The Spruce Woods area provides a unique combination of river-bottom woodlands, stands of conifers, mixed woods and sand dunes interspersed with prairie. Elsewhere, scattered throughout the region, are isolated sand hills of varying size. These tracts of sand, unsuitable for cultivation, are generally wooded and give some local variation to the surrounding terrain.

There are two large water bodies in the southwest corner of the region —Oak Lake and Whitewater Lake. The wetlands bordering these lakes are good habitat for marsh birds.

The nineteen-eighties have been very dry years with minimal spring runoff. Since the early nineteen-eighties water levels have steadily decreased. In 1988 and 1989 extreme drought caused a number of wetlands to dry up completely. This is reflected along several of the routes. Perhaps most notable is Whitewater Lake, which became totally dry in May 1988. The Oak Lake/Plum Marshes have also experienced low water levels with large areas being entirely dry. Above normal precipitation over consecutive years is needed to restore wetlands to their former water levels.

When to come

Each season offers a variety of birding opportunities. By mid-February the early Horned Larks have usually arrived. Through March, Canada Geese, Northern Harriers, American Crows and Mountain Bluebirds may be seen while such winter birds as Snowy Owls, Snow Buntings and Redpolls are still present. April sees the return of raptors and waterfowl while May is noteworthy for numbers of migrating shorebirds and passerines. June and July (particularly June) are the best months for observing the breeding birds of the region. Although "migrant" shorebirds are present from May to October, fall migration is already well underway by July for shorebirds and some passerines. September and October are the best months for viewing impressive numbers of Sandhill Cranes and waterfowl, particularly Snow Geese. November sees the passage of most Bald Eagles through the region and the arrival from the north of winter birds such as Northern Goshawk, Gyrfalcon, Snowy Owl and the winter finches.

One swallow does not make a summer, but one skein of geese cleaving the murk of a March thaw, is the spring.

—Aldo Leopold

Where to stay

The City of Brandon offers a wide variety of accommodation for visiting birders. Most of the smaller towns have at least one motel. For free literature and information on travel and accommodation, including campgrounds, write to:

TRAVEL MANITOBA
Department 7020
7th Floor
155 Carlton Street
Winnipeg, Manitoba
R3C 3H8

1-800-665-0040

or

THE BRANDON ECONOMIC DEVELOPMENT BOARD
Box 1417
Brandon, Manitoba
R7A 6N2

(204) 728-3287

Weather and what to bring

The climate of southwestern Manitoba is continental, generally being quite warm in summer and quite cold in winter. Temperature extremes of +40°C (104°F) in July to -40°C (-40°F) in January have been recorded. June is typically the wettest month of the year, November the driest. In Brandon the average annual precipitation is 450 millimetres (18 inches).

The transition months of April and September can produce very hot and dry, very wet or even snowy weather. Heavy jackets and sweaters are advisable for early spring and late fall birding as are gloves and warm footwear. Rubber boots are handy when birding in the vicinity of wetlands. A rainjacket can be a useful article to carry with you, as summer thunderstorms can occur in short order.

Mosquitoes and black flies, wood ticks and poison ivy can cause some irritation. Insect repellent may be in order, particularly during the early morning and evening hours. Wood ticks occur mainly in May and June. Learn to recognize poison ivy and avoid it. "Leaflets three, let it be." There are no poisonous snakes in Manitoba.

Windy weather is frequently experienced in southwestern Manitoba. The best time for birding, especially for grassland species, is in the early morning hours. Conditions are generally calm and bird activity is at its daily peak.

A note of caution — roads and vehicle trails without gravel can become impassable with wet weather. It's a good idea to "look before you leap."

Some helpful publications

Cleveland, Norman J. et al. Birder's Guide to Southeastern Manitoba. Eco Series No. 1. Manitoba Naturalists Society. Winnipeg. 1988.

Farrand, John, Jr. (editor). The Audubon Society Master Guide to Birding. Three volumes. Knopf, New York. 1983.

Godfrey, W. Earl. The Birds of Canada. Revised edition. National Museum of Natural Sciences. Ottawa. 1986.

Knapton, Richard W. Birds of the Gainsborough-Lyleton Region (Saskatchewan and Manitoba). Special Publication No. 10. Saskatchewan Natural History Society. Regina. 1979.

Manitoba Avian Research Committee (compiler). Field Checklist of the Birds of Manitoba. Manitoba Museum of Man and Nature and Manitoba Naturalists Society. Winnipeg. 1986.

McNicholl, Martin K. Manitoba Bird Studies, 1744-1983: A Bibliography. Manitoba Department of Natural Resources and Manitoba Museum of Man and Nature. Winnipeg. 1985.

Peterson, Roger Tory. Eastern Birds. 4th edition. (a field guide). 1980.

Robbins, C.S. et al. A Guide to Field Identification. Birds of North America. Revised edition. Golden Press, New York. 1983.

Scott, S.L. (editor). Field Guide to the Birds of North America. Second edition. National Geographic Society, Washington. 1987.

Weedon, Daniel (compiler). Birds of Riding Mountain National Park & Region. Checklist. Riding Mountain National Park Interpretive Centre, Wasagaming. Revised 1987.

Local contacts and organizations

		Telephone — area code 204
Brandon:	Jean Horton	728-4672
	Barbara Robinson	728-4029
	David Barnes	728-6278
Carberry:	Bob and Rae Anderson	834-2284
Erickson:	Dan and Thuraya Weedon (Riding Mountain Nature Tours)	636-2968
Lyleton:	John and Joan Murray	649-2382
Minnedosa:	Cal Cuthbert	867-5981
Pierson:	Ralph and Mary Wang	634-2465
Reston:	David L. and Irma Braddell	877-3983
Rivers:	Norman Short	328-7107
Shoal Lake:	Cliff Findlay	759-2506

Brandon Natural History Society, c/o Mrs. A. E. Shuttleworth, 609 McDiarmid Drive, Brandon, Mb. R7B 2H6. Telephone (204) 727-2995.

B.J. Hales Museum of Natural History, Brandon University Campus. Telephone (204) 727-7307.

Manitoba Naturalists Society, 302 - 128 James Avenue, Winnipeg, Mb. R3B 0N8. Telephone (204) 943-9029.

Abbreviations

AGM	Alexander-Griswold Marsh
DM	Douglas Marsh
Km	Kilometre
MPC	Minnedosa Pothole Country
OL/PM	Oak Lake/Plum Marshes
PP	Provincial Park
PR	Provincial Road
PTH	Provincial Trunk Highway
RMNP	Riding Mountain National Park
SW	Spruce Woods
TMPP	Turtle Mountain Provincial Park
WMA	Wildlife Management Area

Metric conversion

1 hectare = 2.5 acres
1 metre = 39.37 inches
1 kilometre = 0.6 mile
Temperatures are in degrees Celsius (°C); °C = 5/9 (°F - 32), °F = 9/5°C + 32

Maps and photographs

Maps

Photographs

Spruce Woods Area **Cal Cuthbert**

Pelican Lake **Cal Cuthbert**

Wetland in Turtle Mountain **Cal Cuthbert**

Whitewater Lake Shoreline **Cal Cuthbert**

Native mixed-grass prairie near Lyleton Cal Cuthbert

Riding Mountain National Park Brian Joynt

River-bottom woodlands along Pembina River   Cal Cuthbert

Slough near Brandon   Mamie McCowan

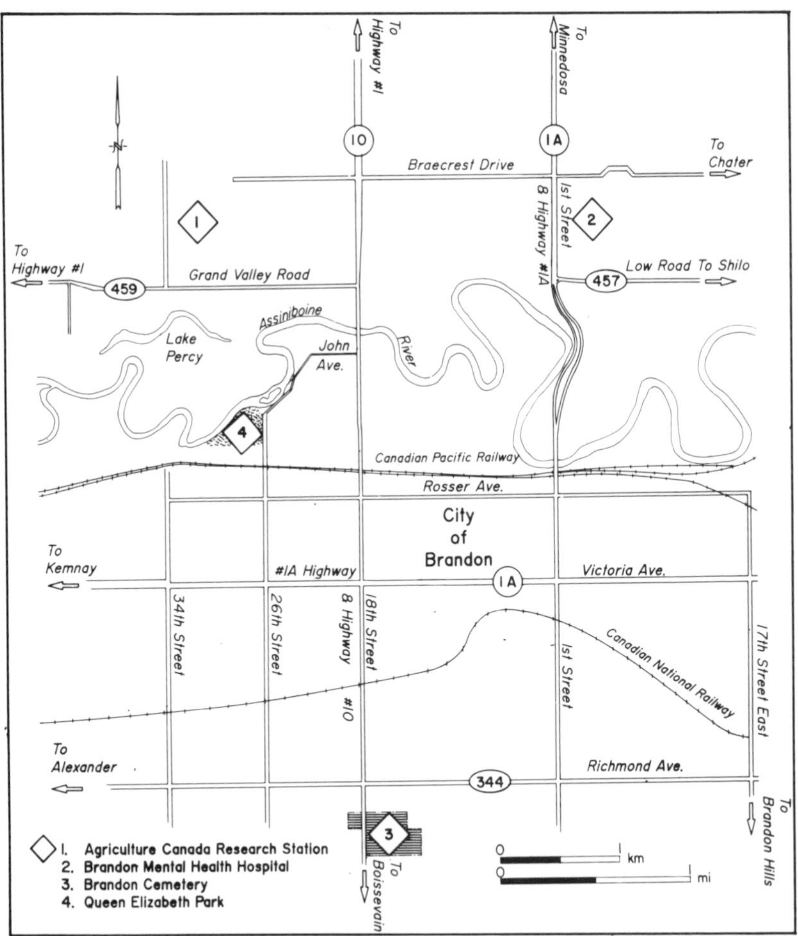

M2 CITY OF BRANDON BIRDING SITES

BIRDING IN BRANDON (M2)

For birders with limited time and/or restricted means of travel, four of the better birding sites within the city limits of Brandon are herein described. These are the Agriculture Canada Research Station, Brandon Mental Health Centre, Brandon Cemetery and Queen Elizabeth Park. The first three sites are particularly good for winter birding. Birds to watch for then include Boreal Chickadee, Red-breasted Nuthatch, Brown Creeper, Golden-crowned Kinglet, Bohemian Waxwing, Pine Grosbeak, Purple Finch, Red and White-winged Crossbills, Common and Hoary Redpolls and Evening Grosbeak. Brandon can be easily traversed from one end to the other by vehicle in less than fifteen minutes.

Agriculture Canada Research Station

The Brandon Experimental Farm was established in 1886 to gather information for the agricultural sector. However, due to co-operative programs involving a number of research centres, the Experimental Farm was reclassified as a Research Station in 1966. The station itself presently encompasses 708 hectares of land and lies partly in the Assiniboine River valley and partly in the uplands.

To reach the Research Station travel 2.4 km north on 18th Street from Rosser Avenue to PR 459 (Grand Valley Road). Turn left and drive 0.8 km to the two stone pillars which mark the entrance to Spruce Drive and the station. Check the small pond on the south side of the road for Wood Duck. As you drive north watch for Merlin. Parking is available at the Main Office Building. Ornamental shrubs, stands of native and exotic conifers and deciduous trees, field crops and colourful flower gardens make this an attractive area for plant lovers as well as birdwatchers. Ruby-throated Hummingbirds frequent the flower gardens. With luck you may see a pair of Gray Partridge along the hedges or field edges. Merlins have nested in the conifers on the grounds of the Director's residence east of the parking lot.

Permanent bird residents include Downy and Hairy Woodpeckers, Blue Jay, Black-billed Magpie, Black-capped Chickadee and White-breasted Nuthatch. Eastern Screech-Owl, Northern Hawk Owl and Barred Owl have been seen in winter.

Brandon Mental Health Centre

The grounds of this large institute are extensively treed, with mature conifers predominating. To reach this site from PR 457, drive north on First Street (1A). The first turn to your right is the main entrance. Follow this road for approximately 100 metres to the parking lot on the right hand side. The area can be quickly checked from here or by walking down the road. Merlins have nested in the mature conifers. Follow the road east and north for about 1 km to a gravel road. Turn left to return to First Street.

Brandon Cemetery

This is Brandon's oldest cemetery and as such supports mature trees including many spruce. From Richmond Avenue drive south on 18th Street (PTH 10) for approximately 0.8 km. The main entrance is to your left. Watch for Merlin here winter or summer. Eastern Screech-Owl, Northern Saw-whet Owl and Black-backed Woodpecker have occurred in winter.

Queen Elizabeth Park

Situated along the Assiniboine River this park includes picnic tables, firewood, barbecues and washroom facilities. Walking trails wind along the river bank through river-bottom woods and willow thickets.

To reach the park from Rosser Avenue and 18th Street, go north for 1.2 km to the dyke road along the south side of the Assiniboine River. Turn west along the dyke road for 1 km past the participark area to the main parking area. Here one can often find many thrushes, vireos, warblers and sparrows in migration. Summer birds include Least Flycatcher, Gray Catbird, Yellow-throated Vireo, Yellow Warbler, Rose-breasted Grosbeak and Northern Oriole. Watch for Wood Duck and Northern Rough-winged Swallow along the river.

BRANDON AREA ROUTES

Route 1 (M3)

East Brandon

This route is approximately 20 km.

From the corner of 17th Street East and Victoria Avenue drive east 1.6 km. The Manitoba Hydro Thermal Electric Generating Station lies to the north. Turn left to the Assiniboine River and the dam. A walk east along the river through river-bottom woodland should produce Warbling Vireo, Rose-breasted Grosbeak and Northern Oriole. In winter the open water should be checked for waterfowl, which could include Mallard, Lesser Scaup, Common Goldeneye.

Return to Victoria Avenue and continue east. The City of Brandon garbage dump lies to the right. In April and May this is a good spot to check for Ring-billed, California and other gulls. Continue east on Victoria Avenue to the railroad crossing. Park here and walk southeast along the railroad track. Check the sloughs to the south for American Bittern, Black-crowned Night-Heron, American Avocet, Willet and, with luck, a Great Egret. Northern Harrier, Great Horned Owl and Short-eared Owl frequent the area. Return to your car and proceed to 49th Street East. Turn right and go 1.6 km to PR 344, scanning the water-filled gravel pits enroute. In winter check for Northern Shrike. Turn left and drive for 1.6 km, watching for Gray Partridge. Nest boxes on fence posts along Route 1 are mostly occupied by Tree Swallows. Go south for 1.6 km. Turn left and drive east for 0.8 km through a ridge of native mixed-grass prairie. Check the shallow wetland for Common Snipe and Wilson's Phalarope. Birds found on this prairie pasture include Upland Sandpiper, Marbled Godwit, Sharp-tailed Grouse, Baird's Sparrow, Chestnut-collared Longspur and Western Meadowlark. The gravel pits to the north provide nesting sites for Bank Swallows. The rough road allowance trail east leads to the Assiniboine River.

From this native mixed-grass prairie site go west for 1.6 km. The pasture to the right should be checked for Sharp-tailed Grouse and Sprague's Pipit. Clay-coloured and Vesper Sparrows occur along the fenceline. Listen for Le Conte's Sparrow in moist grassy spots along this road and Bobolink on higher ground. To return to Brandon follow the road west to PTH 10.

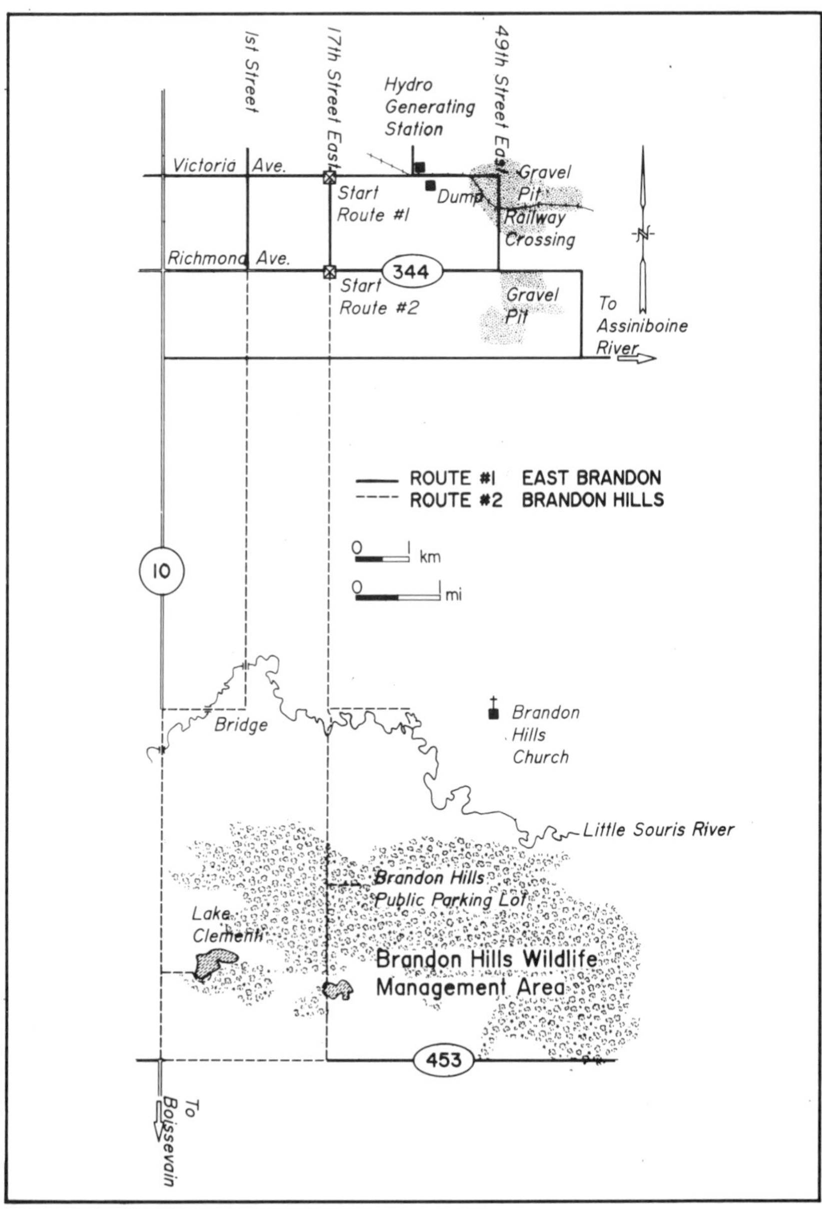

M3 ROUTE # 1 EAST BRANDON
ROUTE # 2 BRANDON HILLS

Route 2 (M3)

Brandon Hills

This route is approximately 40 km.

From 17th Street East and Richmond Avenue in east Brandon travel south, watching for Gray Partridge and Sharp-tailed Grouse along roadside ditches. In early March some of the first returning Mountain Bluebirds are a possibility. At 8.0 km turn left and follow the road which parallels the Little Souris River for 1.6 km. Species to watch for include Wood Duck, Great Horned Owl and Eastern Wood-Pewee. Drive back 1.6 km and continue south for 0.5 km. Check at the bridge for a possible Belted Kingfisher and continue south 2.6 km to the Brandon Hills Wildlife Management Area. Here, turn left and drive towards the parking lot. Ski trails from this point serve as excellent walking trails. Birds to watch for include Black-billed Cuckoo, Great Crested Flycatcher, Yellow-throated Vireo, American Redstart, Rose-breasted Grosbeak and Indigo Bunting. With luck you may see a Scarlet Tanager. Return to your car and upon leaving the parking lot turn left (south) and continue. Check the small lake to your left for Pied-billed and Horned Grebes and waterfowl. The sloughs 0.8 km south of this lake can provide viewing opportunities for several species of ducks, migrant shorebirds and possible American Bittern.

At the corner turn right onto PR 453 and travel 3.2 km to PTH 10. Turn right (north) for 1.6 km, then turn right again to Lake Clementi. In spring and fall this can be a good location for viewing waterfowl, including Tundra Swans and Snow Geese. Return to PTH 10 and continue north for 4.8 km. Turn right and go 0.8 km, stopping at the wooden bridge over the Little Souris River. Eastern Phoebe, Eastern Kingbird, Gray Catbird, Cedar Waxwing, Yellow Warbler, Song Sparrow, Northern Oriole and American Goldfinch are probable sightings. Continue for 0.8 km and turn left. Travelling north on this road for 8.0 km will return you to Brandon. Keep watching for Gray Partridge!

What, is the jay more precious than the lark,
Because his feathers are more beautiful?

—Shakespeare

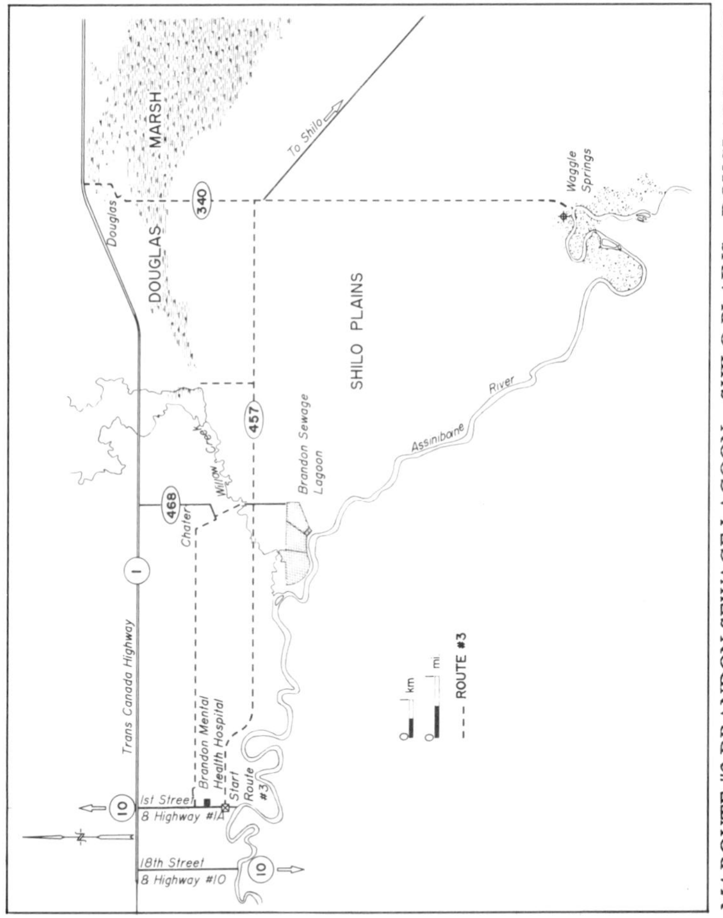

M4 ROUTE #3 BRANDON SEWAGE LAGOON – SHILO PLAINS – DOUGLAS MARSH

Route 3 (M4)

Brandon Sewage Lagoon - Shilo Plains - Douglas Marsh

This route is approximately 63 km.

From the junction of Highway 1A (First Street) and PR 457 drive east from Brandon approximately 8 km. After crossing the bridge over Willow Creek on PR 457 turn right onto a gravel trail which leads south to the Brandon Sewage Lagoon. Watch for Sharp-tailed Grouse along the way. Once at the lagoon turn to your right and drive along the dyke. The large west cell usually has on it a greater number of waterfowl than the other two. This cell also provides excellent opportunities to view waterfowl broods through June and July. During spring and fall migration particularly, there are many species of waterfowl, including Tundra Swans and Snow Geese. With luck you may even spot a Cinnamon Teal, Greater Scaup or Surf Scoter. Migrating shorebirds also occur, including large flocks of Red-necked Phalaropes. Bonaparte's and Ring-billed Gulls are commonly found here but also watch for California Gulls. The wooded banks of Willow Creek along the north side of the west cell offer good birding for many species of songbirds. Belted Kingfisher, Eastern Phoebe and Northern Rough-winged Swallow can be found along the creek banks. Continue on the dyke around the perimeter of the lagoon to turn up such birds as Double-crested Cormorant, Black-crowned Night-Heron and Wood Duck along the Assiniboine River.

Return to PR 457, turn right and proceed 9 km to the Douglas-Shilo junction. Turn right and drive south 8.5 km on the gravel Waggle Springs road, continuing until you reach the Assiniboine River. The remaining undisturbed mixed-grass prairie in this area is home to many prairie bird species, including Upland Sandpiper, Horned Lark, Sprague's Pipit, Vesper, Baird's and Grasshopper Sparrows, Chestnut-collared Longspur and Western Meadowlark. With luck you may spot a Ferruginous Hawk.

Retrace your route to the Douglas-Shilo junction, then continue straight ahead (north) for approximately 2.5 km to the sedge-covered Douglas Marsh. Here you can find many species of marsh birds, including Yellow, Virginia and Sora Rails, Sedge Wren, Le Conte's and Sharp-tailed Sparrows. Douglas Marsh is internationally famous for its Yellow Rails. Their abundance is dependent upon water levels. In 1989 this marsh was dry and supported very few rails. The calls can be heard by visiting the marsh, primarily after dark.

For the fastest route back to Brandon, continue north through Douglas to Highway 1 (Trans-Canada Highway), and turn left. As an alternative route back to Brandon, return to the Douglas-Shilo junction. Turn right and continue for 4.8 km. Turn right again, watching for Gray Partridge, and drive 1.6 km to the west edge of the Douglas Marsh. Sora, Alder Flycatcher, Sedge and Marsh Wrens, Swamp Sparrow and Yellow-headed Blackbird are found here. Bobolinks occur in the meadow to the north of the marsh.

Return to PR 457 and continue on it for 3.2 km. Turn right and drive to the village of Chater. Turn left one block, then turn right to continue to the next municipal road. Turn left. Drive approximately 7.4 km, watching for Loggerhead Shrike, until you reach First Street (1A) at Brandon. The Brandon Mental Health Centre grounds are to your left. This is a good place to check for Merlins.

Route 4 (M5)

Rivers Area and Minnedosa Pothole Country

This route is approximately 126 km.

The starting point is the village of Alexander, approximately 25 km west of Brandon. From this point follow PR 250 north for 8 km. You are now 0.5 km north of the Assiniboine River. Turn left for 6.5 km to an area of rolling, native mixed-grass prairie which is home to Swainson's Hawk, Sharp-tailed Grouse, Upland Sandpiper, Marbled Godwit, Sprague's Pipit and good numbers of Chestnut-collared Longspur. Ferruginous Hawk and Baird's Sparrow have been seen here. Prairie Falcon is occasional in late summer and fall. Snowy Owl may appear in the winter.

For best access to this area turn left for 1.6 km, right for 3.2 km, and again right for 3.2 km. Turn right once more for 9.6 km to PR 250. Yellow Rails have been heard in the marshy area to the right. Turn left on PR 250 for 4 km and listen for Baird's Sparrow in the pasture to the left. Continue for 2.5 km, then turn right for 0.7 km. On the left side of the road is a small area of native prairie where Sprague's Pipit, Baird's and Grasshopper Sparrows and Chestnut-collared Longspur usually nest.

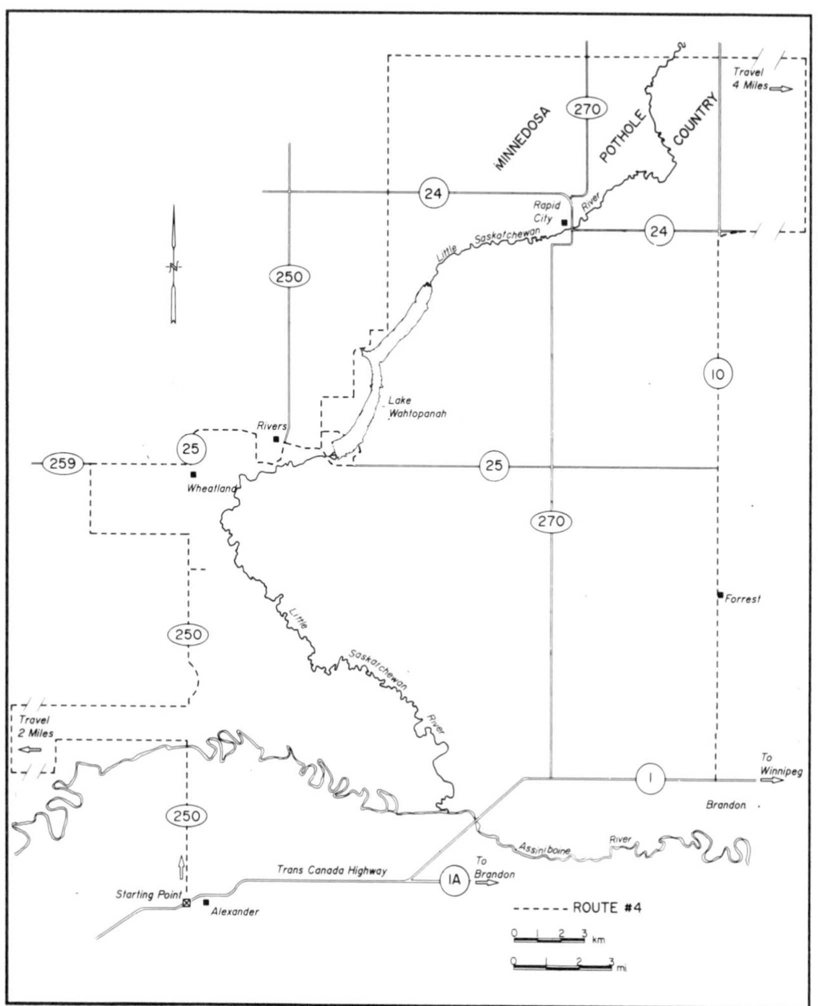

M5 ROUTE #4 RIVERS AREA AND MINNEDOSA POTHOLE COUNTRY

Return to PR 250 and continue travelling north for 1.6 km, turn left for 4.8 km, watching for Loggerhead Shrike, then right for 1.2 km. The ravine is a good spot for Wood Duck and occasionally Western Wood-Pewee. Continue another 2 km, then right for 4.8 km to PTH 25. Turn left onto PTH 25 and travel north on it for 1.6 km, then east 2 km. Turn right on the gravel road just before the railroad tracks and follow it east 1.2 km, then right for 1.2 km. The river-bottom forest in front of you can be a good area for Black-and-white Warbler and Northern Waterthrush. Turn left and follow the winding road east and north for 2 km. Turn right and follow this road 0.6 km to PTH 25. Turn right and travel east out of Rivers for 1.5 km, turn left by the curve for 0.8 km, then right onto pavement for 1.2 km to Lake Wahtopanah Provincial Park. Here is a camping and picnicking area. In early fall watch for migrating warblers. Bald Eagles stop over by the lake in late fall. A good place to look for eagles is from Daly Beach on the south side of the lake. This beach can be reached by following PTH 25 east out of Rivers for 3.5 km and turning left at this point toward the lake. Check for roosting Bald Eagles across the lake on the northwest shore. Look for waterfowl in late fall. Greater Scaup, Oldsquaw and Surf and White-winged Scoters have been seen here.

From the provincial park follow the paved road west for 1.2 km, turn right for 1.6 km, right again for 1.6 km. Turn left for 1.6 km. For access to the lake turn east for 0.8 km. Otherwise continue north and east on a winding road for 3.2 km. At this point there is a dirt trail about 200 metres long leading to the lake. American White Pelican may be seen here, especially to the north on the west shore. Snow Geese can be seen in large numbers in migration, especially in October. Watch for shorebirds along this shoreline in fall migration.

Return to the road and drive north for 13 km, crossing PTH 24. This leads into the Minnedosa pothole country, a North American "hot spot" for breeding waterfowl. Over a dozen species of ducks regularly nest in this region. In recent years Canada Geese have begun nesting here. Other species to look for in the Minnedosa pothole country include Horned Grebe, American Bittern, Virginia Rail, Marsh Wren, Yellow-headed Blackbird. Listen for Le Conte's and Sharp-tailed Sparrows and Sedge Wren in moist grassy areas next to the sloughs along the way. Turn right for 23 km to PR 262, crossing PR 270 and PTH 10. Turn right for 8 km, right again for 6.4 km to PTH 10. Turn left to return to Brandon, a distance of 26 km.

SITE GUIDES

Site 1 (M6)

Spruce Woods Area

Some twenty thousand years ago Manitoba was covered by glacial ice. As the years passed, a warming trend occurred, melting the ice. As a result, Lake Agassiz was formed. A great river, now the Assiniboine, emptied into it and created a huge sand and gravel delta. For a brief time the delta was a sea of wind-blown sand, but soon plants began to move in. The delta was first colonized by conifers — spruce, juniper and tamarack. As the temperatures warmed and the land dried, grasses, shrubs and wildflowers began to grow. In the valley, elm, basswood, ash and Manitoba maple found cooler habitat. Aspen and oak invaded the uplands.

In this guide the Spruce Woods area is defined as being bounded on the south by PTH 2, on the east by PTH 34, on the north by the Trans-Canada Highway and on the west by PR 340. Spruce Woods Provincial Heritage Park occupies 24,576 hectares (61,440 acres) of this area. It is located on PTH 5 between Carberry, just south of the Trans-Canada Highway, and Glenboro on PTH 2. Driving south on PTH 5 watch for Eastern and Mountain Bluebirds and Lark Sparrows. There is a nestbox trail along this road, which provides a splendid opportunity to observe these two species of bluebirds and also Tree Swallows. The Epinette Creek skiing/hiking trail with entrance to the left of PTH 5 is a good place to bird. There is a sign which indicates the start of this trail. Check the spruce for Boreal Chickadee, Red-breasted Nuthatch, Golden-crowned Kinglet and Red and White-winged Crossbills.

As you descend into the Assiniboine River valley, Marsh's Lake can be seen on your right. Wood Ducks are frequently seen from here. Turn in at the sign to Marsh's Lake picnic area. This is a good stopping place for some birding on the Marsh's Lake Trail. A Pileated Woodpecker may be a highlight. Where the trail closely follows the lake, watch for Eared and Red-necked Grebes, Wood Duck, Hooded Merganser and Belted Kingfisher.

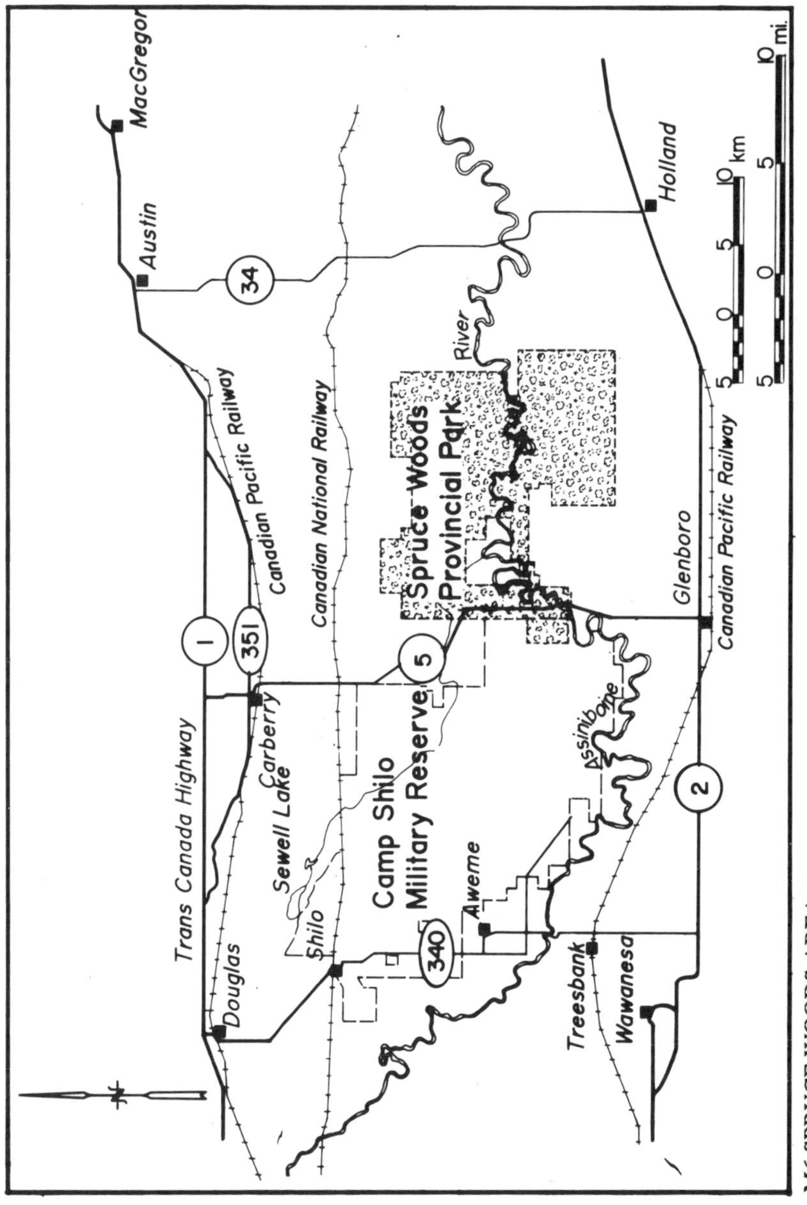

M6 SPRUCE WOODS AREA

Just before reaching the bridge on PTH 5, turn right into the Spirit Hills Intrepretive Trail parking lot. A footpath winds through deciduous and mixed woods, active and stabilized sand dunes and in places follows along the Assiniboine River valley. Birds found here include Turkey Vulture, Orange-crowned Warbler, Scarlet Tanager, Rose-breasted Grosbeak, Indigo Bunting, Rufous-sided Towhee, Red and White-winged Crossbills. Adjoining the Spirit Hills trail is another leading to the Devil's Punch Bowl. The turquoise pools of water in the punch bowl were created by beaver damming the springs flowing into the bowl.

Continue south on PTH 5, crossing the Ernest Thompson Seton bridge over the Assiniboine River. Northern Rough-winged Swallows may be seen near the river. Turn left onto the road leading to Spruce Woods campground and picnic area. Brochures are available at the campground office. Watch for Broad-winged Hawks. The Isputinaw Trail is reached from the road into the picnic area. The trail traverses moist woodland, a creek, boggy wetland and dry upland slopes. Alder Flycatchers frequent the vicinity of the boardwalk. Leaving the picnic area, return to the gravel road and travel east watching for signs pointing to Steel's Ferry Overlook and Springridge Trail. Indigo Buntings are often seen along the way. The trail descends through moist woodland to the Assiniboine River level and back up. Northern Goshawk has nested east of this location.

Upon returning to PTH 5, go south (left) and drive to the sign indicating the turn to the Interpretive Centre. Exhibits depicting features of the park are found here, as is the "Spirit Sands" book shop operated by the "Friends of Spruce Woods". Watch for Turkey Vultures overhead.

The species mentioned as occurring along PTH 5 and adjacent roads are representative of birds found in the Spruce Woods area.

A return to Brandon can be made by taking either PTH 2 west from Glenboro or PTH 1 (Trans-Canada Highway) west from Carberry. If returning to Brandon via Carberry, PR 351 west through the town offers a scenic drive. Red-headed Woodpecker, Eastern and Mountain Bluebirds and Rufous-sided Towhee may be spotted along this route.

Site 2 (M7 and M8)

Tri-Lakes (Pembina River Valley)

For purposes of this guide the Pembina River valley is defined as extending from Bone Lake in the northwestern corner to Swan Lake in the east. Throughout this area the generally U-shaped valley is from 2 to 3.2 km wide and approximately 61 metres deep. A number of deep wooded ravines occur tributary to the valley along this reach. In the past the streams in these ravines have deposited sediments over the valley floor which now act as natural dams across the valley. These natural dams have resulted in the formation of Bone, Overend, Grassy, Pelican, Lorne, Louise, Rock and Swan Lakes (M7). The largest of these are Pelican, Rock and Swan Lakes, hence the local name of Tri-Lakes.

The Pembina River valley provides some of the most beautiful scenery in southwestern Manitoba. Bur oak is dominant on southern exposures. Elsewhere, including the flat bottomlands of the valley floor, green ash, Manitoba maple, white elm, white birch and trembling aspen are found. The variety of habitats present offers an interesting cross-section of birding opportunities.

The following is a route around Pelican Lake (M8). The better part of a day will be required to bird the route as described here, particularly if one is commuting from Brandon. Pelican Lake, the largest of the tri-lakes, is the most accessible and is representative of the birding to be found throughout this reach of the scenic Pembina River valley.

The majority of access routes to the shores of Pelican Lake are herein described. These lead to cottage developments and during the summer months there can be more people than birds, especially on weekends. April, May and September are the best times to bird these sites, particularly for migrating waterbirds and passerines. October and November are good months to view Bald and, to a lesser extent, Golden Eagles as they migrate down the valley.

Drive south on PTH 18 through the Tiger Hills to Ninette. Upon entering the valley just north of Ninette you will see a Pembina Valley Wildlife Management Area sign on the east side of the road just north of the small bridge. To the southeast of this sign is Grassy Lake. The wet meadows here are worth checking for Sedge Wrens, Le Conte's and Sharp-tailed Sparrows. Alder Flycatchers frequent the willow clumps east of these meadows. The north end of Grassy

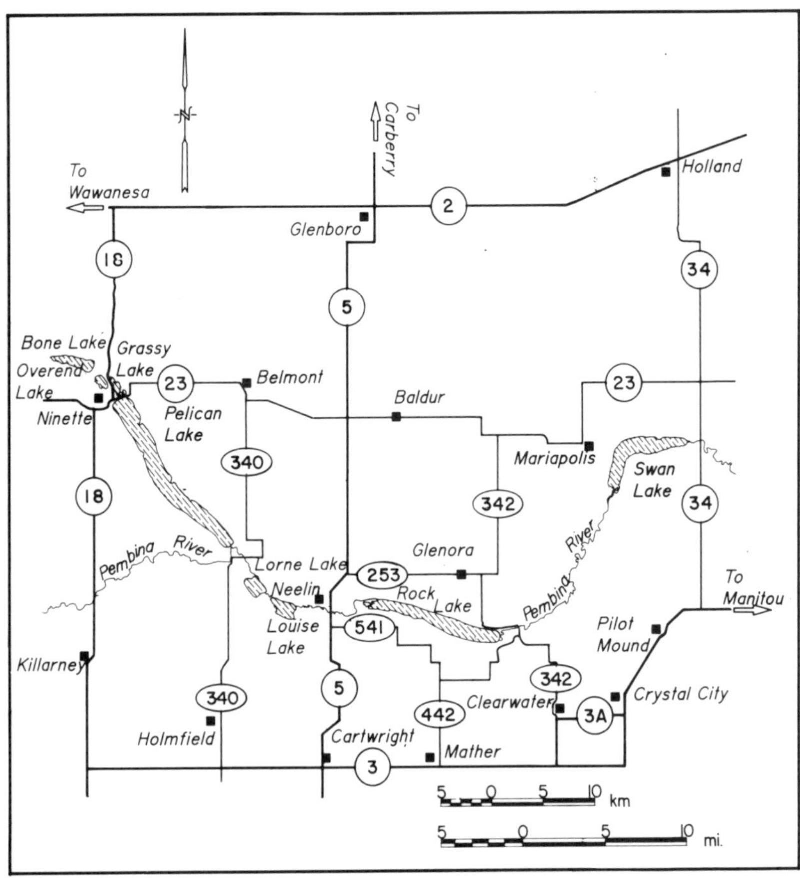

M7 TRI-LAKES (PEMBINA RIVER VALLEY)

Lake is dominated by cattail and in most years supports good numbers of Marsh Wrens. The full length of Grassy Lake can be viewed by continuing south on PTH 18 towards Ninette. This is a fine area for staging waterfowl in mid to late summer and can be especially good for Tundra Swans through October. Some American White Pelicans frequent the basin through the summer months. Continue south through the village of Ninette to Lake Street. Turn left to Argyle Street, then right to the lakeshore. Clark's Grebes have nested in the bulrush at this location. From here turn around and drive north through Ninette to PTH 23. Turn right and drive east along the north shore of Pelican Lake, watching for grebes, waterfowl and other waterbirds. Here in years of normal water levels Western Grebes often nest in loose colonies among the bulrush beds. Dancing birds may frequently be seen in May and early June. This is also a good area to watch for Great Egrets and other southern herons.

After crossing the cement bridge at the east side of the lake turn right at the Pelican Lake Training Centre and drive south on the winding road which parallels the lake. Northern Rough-winged Swallows have nested in the shale embankments on the east side of the road. Follow this road east for 1 km, turn right at the yield sign and drive south for 1.6 km. This takes you to Manhattan Beach. In spring and again in fall this point can be a good place to bird. The gravel/rock tip of this point is a resting area for waterbirds, including American White Pelicans, Double-crested Cormorants and gulls. This is private property so please respect all signs.

From Manhattan Beach turn east and drive 1.6 km, then right for 1 km. Rufous-sided Towhee and Lark Sparrow occur along the wooded ravine slopes in this area. Continue south then east for 1.6 km. Watch for Sharp-tailed Grouse and Eastern Bluebirds. Again turn right and drive 3.2 km. At this point continue south for 1 km to Strathcona Park. This area is generally productive for viewing waterbirds.

From Strathcona Park drive east for 1.6 km, then turn south. By continuing south on this road Cow Point will be reached. The best birding here is along the winding road leading to Cow Point. Rufous-sided Towhees occur on these predominantly oak and ash-covered slopes.

Return to the Cow Point/Strathcona Park road junction, turn right, crossing the wooded ravine, and drive east 3.2 km to a junction in the road. Small sloughs near this junction can be checked for waterfowl. Turn right and drive

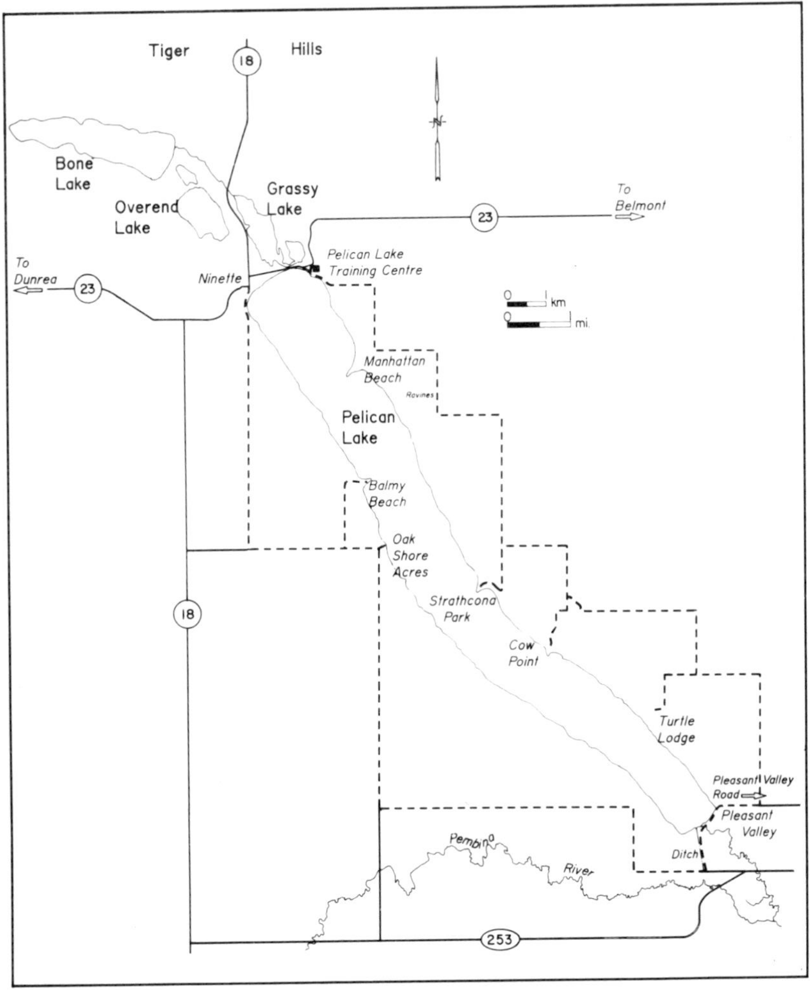

M8 PELICAN LAKE

1.6 km. Access to the lake is possible by turning right again and following the road to the Turtle Lodge developments.

Otherwise, from this junction proceed east for 1.6 km, then south for 3.2 km to the Pleasant Valley Road. Turn right to reach Pleasant Valley. Red-headed Woodpeckers frequent this end of Pelican Lake. The gravel beach should be checked for shorebirds, especially in August and September. Franklin's, Bonaparte's, Ring-billed and occasionally California and Herring Gulls occur. With luck, you may see Caspian and Common Terns. A fair-weather trail continues along the north side of the golf course and parallels the Pembina River drainage ditch south to a gravel road. Turn right. For 1.8 km the road follows the steep Pembina River valley. Listen for Veery, Rose-breasted Grosbeak, Indigo Bunting and Rufous-sided Towhee. Follow the road north and west for 8.0 km. Turn north and drive 4.6 km. Check over the pasture to your left for Sharp-tailed Grouse and Sprague's Pipit. Eastern and Mountain Bluebirds may also be seen in the brushy pastureland in this area. Continue north to the bend in the road. By driving straight ahead across the Texas gate and following the road, Oak Shore Acres can be reached. Eastern Wood-Pewee and Yellow-throated Vireo occur among the taller mature trees.

Balmy Beach can be reached by continuing west at the bend in the road (instead of crossing the gate) and driving 0.8 km. Turn north and drive 1.6 km. This point is another good place from which to view waterbirds, including migrating waterfowl.

To reach Ninette from here return south for 1.6 km to the east-west road, turn right and drive west for 2.4 km. Turn right again and drive north for 6.4 km.

Site 3 (M9)

Turtle Mountain Provincial Park

Turtle Mountain Provincial Park, in the southwest corner of the province, can be reached by driving 100 km south of Brandon or approximately 15 km south of the town of Boissevain on PTH 10. Part of the park is on the Canada-United States border where it meets the International Peace Garden, famous for its beautiful flower gardens. Turtle Mountain is covered with about one-third water and two-thirds deciduous forest. It rises 180 to 245 metres above the prairie.

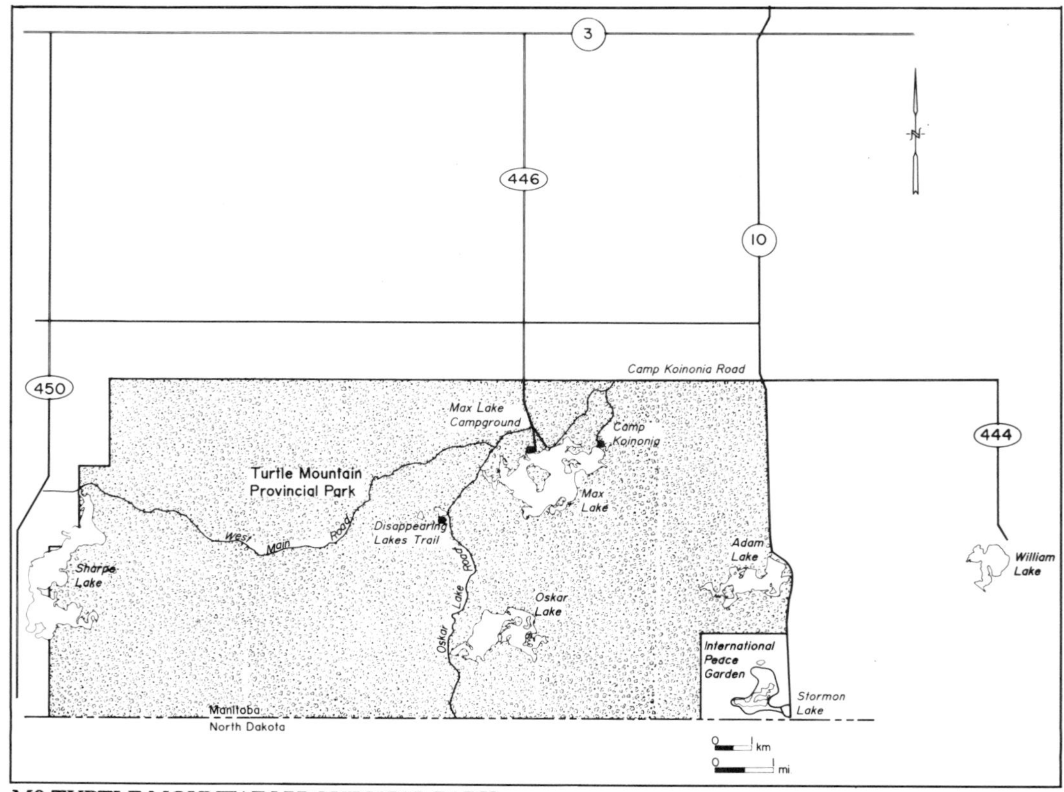

M9 TURTLE MOUNTAIN PROVINCIAL PARK

Wetlands in the area vary from small sloughs to large lakes and are generally shallow with the main source of water being precipitation. Forest and wetland bird species are plentiful in the park. Grassland and agricultural habitats just outside the park are home to additional species of prairie birds. Trembling aspen, balsam poplar, green ash, bur oak, white elm, Manitoba maple and birch make up the deciduous forest while dogwood, willow and hazelnut are the common shrubs of the area. Many white spruce plantings occur, some mature and others younger.

Campgrounds are located at Adam Lake and Max Lake in the park and at William Lake just east of the park. Hiking and ski trails are located in the Adam Lake area where you can choose from a short trail of 2.5 km, longer trails such as the James Lake Trail of 15 km or Adam Lake Trail of 10km. In the campground area and on the trails watch for Great Crested Flycatcher, Rose-breasted Grosbeak and Indigo Bunting. Although not of regular occurrence Northern Parula and Northern Cardinal have nested in the Adam Lake area.

The Max Lake area may be reached by driving 10 km south of the junction of PTH 10 and PTH 3, and 7 km west along the Camp Koinonia Road located at the park's northern boundary. After you have driven 4 km west on the Camp Koinonia Road towards Max Lake make several stops along the roadside looking for deciduous woods with thick shrub understory. Here you should look and listen for Broad-winged Hawk, Black-billed Cuckoo, Alder and Least Flycatchers, Yellow-throated Vireo, Indigo Bunting and several species of warblers including Chestnut-sided, Black-and-white and Mourning.

A campground and a day use area are located at Max Lake as well as access to two canoe routes. Many of the roads and trails in the park are dry-weather roads in summer and snowmobile trails in winter and caution is advised in driving them. Oskar Lake Road and West Main Road are accessible from Max Lake and lead to many sloughs and lakes. These can be checked for Common Loon, Double-crested Cormorant, Black-crowned Night-Heron, Ring-necked Duck and Hooded Merganser. White spruce plantings along the road should be checked for boreal forest species such as Red-breasted Nuthatch, Ruby-crowned Kinglet, Cape May and Yellow-rumped Warblers, which have all been observed in these spruce. In winter these conifers have produced Brown Creeper, Pine Grosbeak, Purple Finch and Red Crossbill. Large thatching ant hills may be observed in the vicinity of the spruce plantings.

The Disappearing Lakes Trail is located by driving 3 km south from PR 446 along the Oskar Lake Road. It is one and a half km in length. A short hike along a boardwalk and through the marsh will take about one hour and should produce nesting Red-necked Grebes, Hooded Mergansers and numerous water-fowl species. As you leave the Max Lake area go north on PR 446 checking the spruce stands just before the park boundary for boreal forest species. Just outside the park boundary on this same road Eastern Bluebirds are frequently found nesting in natural cavities.

Maps and brochures of Turtle Mountain Provincial Park are available at the park office at Adam Lake or by writing Turtle Mountain Provincial Park, Box 820, Boissevain, Manitoba R0K 0E0.

Site 4 (M10)

Whitewater Lake

Situated between the towns of Boissevain to the east and Deloraine to the west, Whitewater Lake is a unique geographical feature of southwestern Manitoba. This extensive saline lake is characterized by its large open water zone with a fringe of emergent vegetation, poorly defined shoreline, an "island" extending into the lake on its north side and areas of shallow marsh off the east end and southwest corner.

While the immediate topography surrounding the lake is flat to gently rolling, to the south Turtle Mountain rises to 228 metres above the lake in a

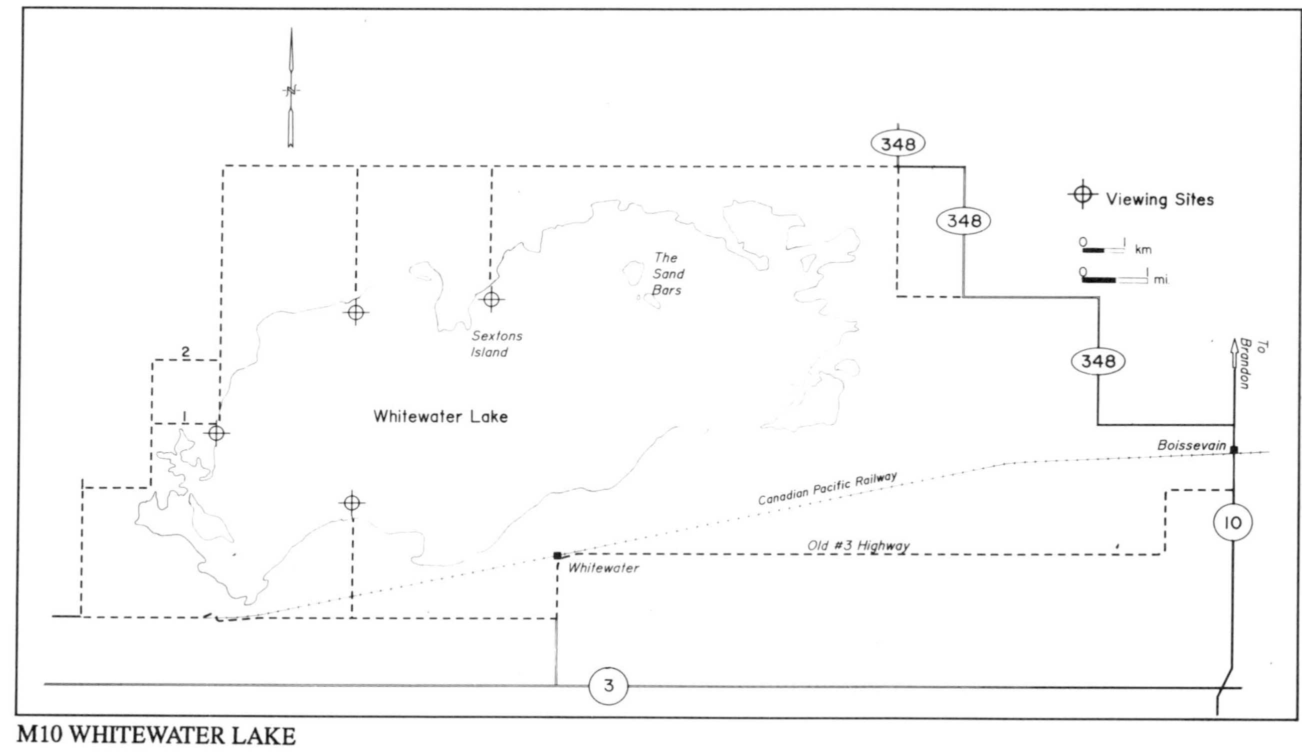

M10 WHITEWATER LAKE

horizontal distance of about 16 km. It is from Turtle Mountain that the lake receives most of its water in the form of runoff. PTH 3 to the south of Whitewater Lake crosses these natural channels or drains, several of which are heavily wooded.

Whitewater Lake is subject to extreme fluctuations in water levels. While it has dried up completely during extreme drought, once in the early thirties and again in 1988 and 1989, it can hold up to 10,320 hectares of water in high-water years. During such years the lake can exceed 13 km in length, 6 km in width and have a maximum depth of 2.1 metres. Generally it is much shallower with an average depth of just under 1 metre.

Because of the large surface area and shallow depth of the lake, water levels are greatly influenced by wind. A strong west wind can create mudflats along the west side of the lake but raise the water level by as much as 0.3 metre at its east end. This has not only restricted the establishment of emergent vegetation but also keeps the water quite turbid. The fine silts and clays suspended in the water under such conditions give the lake a milky-gray colour.

Whitewater Lake is a relatively "unbirded" area, perhaps because it is largely inaccessible and is a considerable distance from a large urban centre. In years of normal water level this lake is an excellent place to view spectacular numbers of migrating waterfowl, including Tundra Swans and Snow Geese. Greater White-fronted and Ross' Geese can also be seen. Estimates of from 150,000 to 200,000 Snow Geese have been made from mid-September to mid-October in some years. Hundreds of Sandhill Cranes may be seen through September, especially towards the east end of the lake. The generally extensive mudflats provide good opportunities to study shorebirds both in spring and mid to late summer. Hundreds of American Avocets stage here.

A full day is recommended to bird the following route comfortably. From Boissevain take the first road west at the south end of the town (old No. 3) and drive 0.8 km. The creek here can be a good place to check for waterfowl, particularly in April and May. Continue on this road for 0.8 km, turn south 1.6 km, then travel west for 5.6 km. Check the large pasture to your right for Burrowing Owl and Chestnut-collared Longspur. Continue west for 5.4 km. Check the long row of mature cottonwood trees for Red-headed Woodpecker and Western Kingbird. Continue west to the village of Whitewater. Orchard Orioles have nested in the maple trees here. Turn south for 1.6 km, then west for 4.8 km. For access to the lake turn north here. Note — this road is impassable in wet weather. In October thousands of Tundra Swans can be seen to the north and west from this vantage point. Return to the main road and continue west for 3.2 km. Just after crossing the Canadian Pacific railway and bridge, park your vehicle and walk north along the fenceline. This can be a good location to see Swainson's Hawk, Upland Sandpiper, Marbled Godwit and Chestnut-collared Longspur. Sprague's Pipit may be heard. Continue driving west for 3.2 km, then turn north. Check the pasture to your left (west) for Ferruginous Hawk and Burrowing Owl. Continue north for 3.2 km, then turn east 1.6 km. If the road is dry, you can continue east towards the lake for an additional 0.8 km. The areas of marsh vegetation should produce Sedge and Marsh Wrens and Le Conte's and Sharp-tailed Sparrows. With luck you may see a Short-eared Owl. Return 0.8 km, turn right and drive north 1.6 km.

At this point there is a choice of two routes. (1) If the trail to your right is dry, follow it to the lakeshore. A shallow slough to your right is a good place to see waterfowl and shorebirds, including Wilson's Phalarope. By turning north you can follow the lakeshore. This is a good location to scan the lake. In May watch for Peregrine Falcon in this area. Check the pasture to your right for Sprague's Pipit and Chestnut-collared Longspur as you continue north to the road at the completion of 1.6 km. (2) As an alternative to (1), continue north for 1.6 km, turn right for 1.6 km, where both routes meet.

From here drive north for 4.8 km. Turn right and drive 3.2 km. By turning south here the lakeshore can again be reached. Otherwise continue east for an additional 3.2 km. Turn right and travel south to the lakeshore. This is a fair-weather road. Listen for Baird's Sparrow in the extensive weedy marsh meadows enroute. Park your vehicle near the Whitewater Lake Wildlife Management Area sign and follow the trail towards the higher ground known as Sexton's "Island". This is private property so please leave only your footprints. This is one of the few wooded areas adjacent to the lake. In May and September it can be a good site to view migrating warblers and sparrows. Piping Plovers have nested east of this "island" in recent years. Mudflats along the lake here are good for a large assortment of other shorebirds. Watch for California Gulls among the Ring-bills. In late October and November, Bald Eagles are frequently seen in the vicinity of the "island".

Return to the gravel road and continue east for 9.6 km to PR 348. At this point turn right and drive south 3.2 km. Watch for Prairie Falcon, particularly from mid-July through September in the pasture and haylands along this the eastern end of Whitewater Lake. This area is good for staging Sandhill Cranes in September.

At the end of the 3.2 km is an earthen dike. This dike is part of a 1,235-hectare Ducks Unlimited Canada project to improve waterfowl nesting habitat in this region. Turn left and drive east 1.6 km to again reach PR 348. This road will lead you to Boissevain.

Site 5 (M11)

Pipestone-Lyleton-Melita Area

The route described in this site guide provides an overview of the topography and diverse scenery to be found in the southwestern corner of the region. From the flat, mainly cultivated Pipestone plain to local park-like landscapes near Pierson, and from open native mixed-grass pasturelands to extensive field shelterbelts of trees near Lyleton, this area provides habitats for most prairie birds to be found in Manitoba. Combined with the diverse Souris River valley, this area truly becomes the prairie bird mecca of Manitoba. While the majority of prairie species sought by birders may be found in routes closer to Brandon, some, like the Burrowing Owl, Say's Phoebe and Lark Bunting, are most likely to be seen on this route. Although it can be birded in a full day, two days are recommended, especially if combined with the adjacent Oak Lake/Plum Marshes and/or Turtle Mountain routes.

From the junction of PTH 2 and PTH 83, just west of Pipestone, travel south on PTH 83 for 3.2 km. Turn right and drive west for 1.6 km, checking the pasture to your left for Burrowing Owls. This heavily-grazed pasture infested with Richardson's Ground Squirrels is typical of good Burrowing Owl habitat in southwestern Manitoba. Return to PTH 83 and continue south 14.8 km to the junction with PR 345. Watch for Ferruginous Hawks. Turn right onto PR 345 and drive west for 4.8 km. Check the hydro lines for Loggerhead Shrikes. A walk through part of Broomhill Wildlife Management Area to your right should turn up a Sharp-tailed Grouse. Continue west on PR 345 to the junction with PR 252. Turn left onto gravel PR 252 and drive 3.2 km. These pasturelands are part of a region known locally as Poverty Plains due to light soils. In dry years Lark Buntings may be common. Sprague's Pipit, Baird's and Grasshopper Sparrows, and Chestnut-collared Longspur occur annually. There is a good possibility of seeing Ferruginous Hawks here. Continue south to the junction

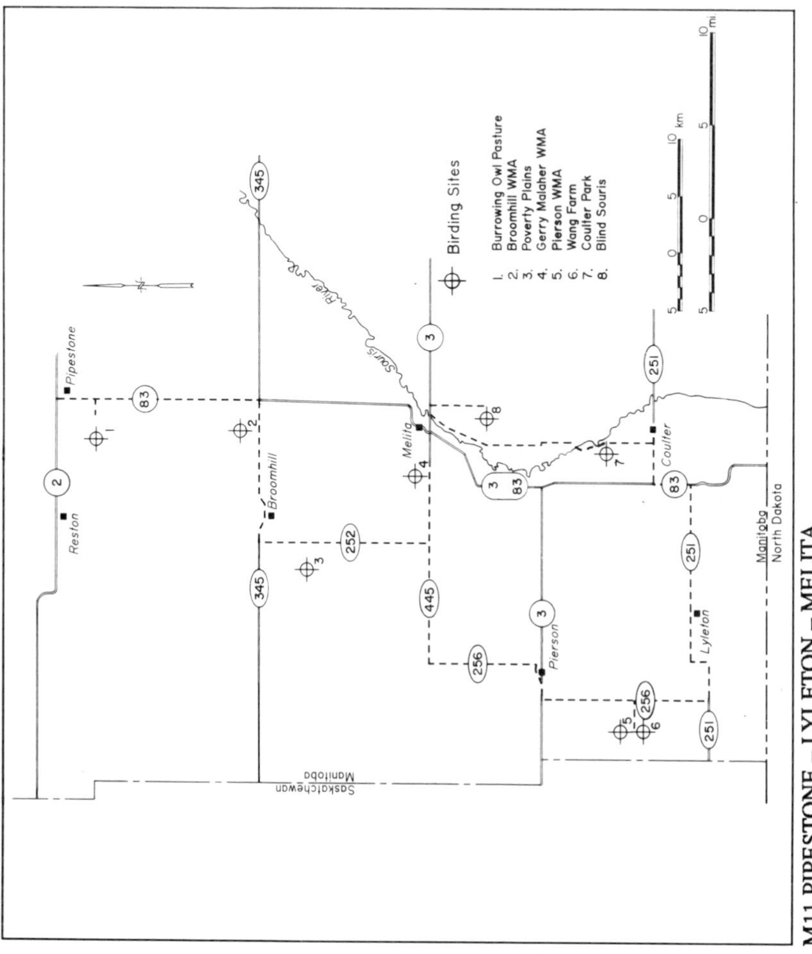

M11 PIPESTONE – LYLETON – MELITA

with PR 445. For some diversity in habitat turn left and drive east 6.4 km towards Melita to the Gerry Malaher Wildlife Management Area. This small but interesting area supports a number of planted conifers, primarily Scots Pine, introduced and native shrubs and even a small dam. Watch for Gray Partridge and Ring-necked Pheasant.

Return to the junction of PR 252 and PR 445 and continue west on PR 445 for 9.6 km to PR 256. Turn left and drive south 9.6 km to Pierson. Turn right onto PTH 3 and drive 2.8 km before turning left onto a gravel road. Follow this road south for 8.0 km. Gray Partridge are common most years in this region. Watch also for Sharp-tailed Grouse which may appear along road and field edges. Turn right onto a fair-weather road and drive west for 2.2 km. The partially wooded area to your right is the Pierson Wildlife Management Area and provides undisturbed habitat for woodland birds, including Long-eared Owl and Black-billed Cuckoo. By continuing west an additional 1.8 km and turning left, the farmsite of Ralph and Mary Wang will be reached. The Ducks Unlimited Canada project on their property provides fine opportunities for viewing a wide variety of waterbirds, including Canada Geese and a dozen species of ducks present through the summer. Greater White-fronted and Ross'Geese are spring and fall visitants. Migrating shorebirds also find the wetland attractive. This is private land. Please ask for permission to bird this property.

From here return east 4.0 km to the gravel road. Turn right and drive 1.6 km to the Gainsborough Creek bridge. With luck you may hear a Willow Flycatcher. Continue south for 4.8 km. The large open pastures with native mixed grasses provide habitat for Upland Sandpiper, Burrowing Owl and other grassland species. Lark Bunting numbers vary considerably from year to year. Watch for Dickcissels. Turn left onto PR 256 and follow it 3.2 km east and 1.6 km north to the junction with PR 251. Turn right onto PR 251. Check the small Ducks Unlimited Canada wetland to your left for waterfowl. Continue east to Lyleton. Say's Phoebes have nested in this village. However, a check on old abandoned farmsites and buildings should turn up a pair of these birds. The planted rows of trees and shrubby roadsides in this area provide habitat for nearly 90% of the population of Loggerhead Shrikes in Manitoba. Orchard Orioles nest in Lyleton and surrounding farmsteads, so you may want to listen for them.

From Lyleton continue east on PR 251 to PTH 83. Turn left onto PTH 83 and drive north 3.2 km, then right again onto PR 251 and drive east 3.2 km, crossing the Antler River enroute. To see the open expanses of the Souris River valley continue east on PR 251 for 3.2 km. Otherwise turn left and drive north for 4.8 km to Coulter Park at the junction of the Antler and Souris Rivers. The woods here offer fine birding in May and again in September for migrating songbirds. Summer residents include Belted Kingfisher, Red-headed Woodpecker (scarce), Eastern Wood-Pewee, Great Crested Flycatcher, Yellow-throated Vireo (scarce) and Rose-breasted Grosbeak. A Black-headed Grosbeak is a possibility. Drive north on this winding road, crossing the Souris River. Watch for Northern Rough-winged Swallows. Continue north for 2.8 km, turn left 0.4 km, then north again to Melita. Lark Sparrows may be found along the partially wooded slopes of the Souris River valley. Once at PTH 83 check the Souris River for Wood Ducks. The oxbow beside PTH 83 to your right should also be checked for Wood Ducks and other waterfowl.

For additional areas in which to search for Willow Flycatchers, drive east on PTH 83 from the Souris River bridge for 1.0 km, then turn right and drive south 4.8 km. Checking small clumps of willows and brush in this interesting region known as the Blind Souris River valley may turn up one of these flycatchers. Here side roads are fair-weather roads and vehicle trails only but may provide additional opportunities for finding not only Willow Flycatchers but other previously-mentioned birds as well.

Brandon can be reached by means of PTH 83 or PTH 3 and associated highways.

Site 6 (M12)

Oak Lake/Plum Marshes

In southwestern Manitoba there are few more enjoyable localities in which to spend a day "prairie birding" than the Oak Lake area. This area provides a good diversity of habitats, including the wide expanse of open water of Oak Lake itself, the narrow treed beach ridge with the wooded "island" of Oak Lake Resort, large marshes, extensive wet meadows, open pastureland and wooded bluffs.

Oak Lake receives most of its water from Pipestone Creek, which enters the lake from the west. Plum Creek is the natural outlet to the southeast. Oak Lake itself typically covers some 2,833 hectares, but with a maximum water depth of 3.0 metres is fairly shallow. A series of shallow wetlands joined together along the northwest side of Oak Lake comprises Oak Lake marsh. To the south of the beach ridge lie the Plum Lakes. For purposes of this guide, the Plum Lakes and adjacent sloughs make up the extensive Plum marshes. Together with Oak Lake and the Oak Lake marsh, approximately 9,000 hectares of lake and marshland exist. Not surprisingly, this area is very attractive to migrating and nesting waterfowl and other marsh birds. A 16,100-hectare Special Canada Goose Refuge is located here.

From Brandon, Oak Lake can be reached by travelling west on the Trans-Canada Highway (Highway #1) past the town of Oak Lake to the junction of Highway #1 and PR 254. However, a more interesting route is to turn south off Highway #1 onto PTH 21 at Griswold. Follow this road south for 3.5 km. The wetlands on either side of the road are the west end of the Alexander-Griswold Marsh. Waterfowl nesting islands may be seen on both sides. While the marsh at this locality has been dry the past few years, it can be a good spot for viewing shorebirds, several species of ducks, and in April and September Tundra Swan and Snow Goose. Continue south for an additional 10 km to the junction with PR 543, watching for Eastern and Mountain Bluebirds enroute. Turn right. The large open pasture to your left is good for Sprague's Pipit. Drive west on PR 543 for 11.2 km. This road passes through the treed Oak Lake Sand Hills. Watch for Broad-winged Hawk, Black-billed Cuckoo, Least Flycatcher, Eastern and Mountain Bluebirds, Rufous-sided Towhee and Lark Sparrow. Turn right and drive north on PR 254 1.6 km, then left to Oak Lake Resort. The pastureland along the north side of the road is frequented by Swainson's Hawk, Upland

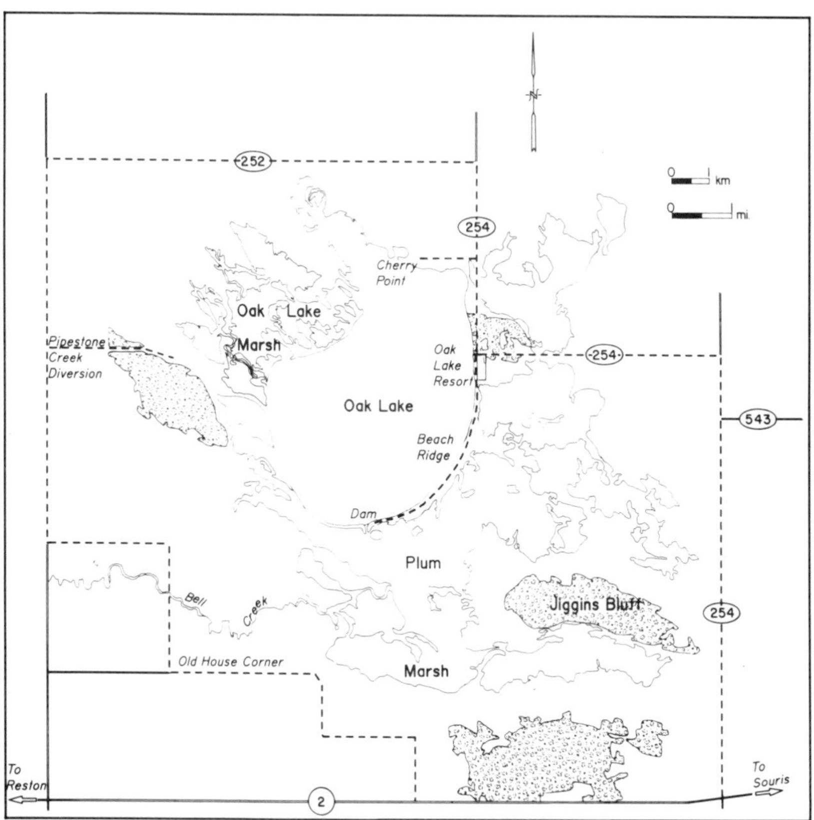

M12 OAK LAKE / PLUM MARSHES

Sandpiper and Marbled Godwit. Cinnamon Teal have been seen along the north ditch.

Oak Lake Resort with acres of bur oak trees is an excellent place to bird for warblers and sparrows in late April and through May. It also provides good fall birding. Species which remain to nest include Eastern Wood-Pewee, Great Crested Flycatcher, Yellow-throated Vireo, Rose-breasted Grosbeak and Northern Oriole. The sandy beaches can be good for shorebirds, depending upon water levels.

To the south of the resort lies the narrow wooded beach ridge. A rough fair-weather road follows the ridge south and west for approximately 5.6 km to a cement dam in a channel which joins the lake with the Plum marshes to the south. Nesting birds include Gray Catbird, Brown Thrasher, Warbling Vireo, Yellow Warbler and occasionally Orchard Oriole. Watch for American Bittern, Black-crowned Night-Heron, Virginia Rail and Common Snipe in and along the ditch which parallels the road. Sedge Wren, Le Conte's and Sharp-tailed Sparrows occur in the wet meadow vegetation to the south of the ditch. The dam is often a good spot from which to view Eared and Western Grebes (watch for Clark's), waterfowl, a variety of shorebirds and Forster's Tern. A large Franklin's Gull colony has existed for several years to the south of this channel in the Plum marshes.

Another good place for viewing Oak Lake is Cherry Point, which can be reached by driving north of the resort on PR 254 for 2.4 km and taking the first road to your left. Follow this road for 1.7 km and through the planted pine trees. This is a good spot for viewing Bald and (with luck) Golden Eagles in late October and November as they prey on straggling waterfowl.

If one still has species to find, a trip around Oak Lake and its marshes may be in order. Follow PR 254 south to PTH 2. South of the PR 254-PR 543 junction check the ditches and wet meadows along the road for waterfowl, Willet, Marbled Godwit, Wilson's Phalarope and other shorebirds. Cliff Swallows nest beneath the two small bridges along this stretch of road. At PTH 2 turn right and drive west 8 km. Turn north onto a gravel road and follow this road as it winds north and west for 10 km to the "old house" corner. Check pastures for Swainson's and, with luck, Ferruginous Hawks. Burrowing Owls have been very local nesters in this region. Baird's Sparrows are most likely to be heard in grassy areas not mowed or heavily grazed. Turn north onto a fair-weather road for 3.2 km, crossing Bell Creek enroute. Chestnut-collared Longspurs occur in the pasture immediately north of the creek to your right and in the large pastures at the end of the 3.2 km. Watch for Loggerhead Shrike along the road allowance shrubbery as you drive north. By turning left and driving west 3.2 km a main north-south municipal road will be reached. The Pipestone Creek Diversion located 3.2 km north on this municipal road is a good place to check for waterfowl, including Wood Duck, and rare egrets. By continuing north for 4.8 km, PR 255 is reached. With luck you may see Sharp-tailed Grouse along the road edge. Turn right and drive east 11.0 km to PR 254. Baird's Sparrows occur in unmown grassy sites along this road. From PR 254, either turn north to Highway #1 or south to Oak Lake Resort.

It will take a full day to thoroughly bird this route.

The reason birds can fly and we can't is simply that they have perfect faith, for to have faith is to have wings.

—J. M. Barrie

Site 7 (M13)

Riding Mountain National Park

In the region covered by this guide Riding Mountain National Park is the best place to find the greatest diversity of bird species; for a few it is the only known location. Two hundred and sixty species of birds have been recorded for Riding Mountain National Park and the surrounding agricultural area just outside the boundary.

Riding Mountain lies 95 km north of the city of Brandon, with the south gate of the park and townsite of Wasagaming located on PTH 10. At Wasagaming, information on nature trails and park nature programs as well as a checklist of birds of Riding Mountain National Park and region are available at the Interpretive Centre.

This is an excellent area to spend several days renewing observations of familiar birds and adding species to a life list. To accommodate visitors there are cabins and motels (book well in advance) as well as a fully-serviced campground in the townsite of Wasagaming. Other campgrounds are located in the park at Lake Katherine, Moon Lake, Lake Audy and Whirlpool Lake.

Riding Mountain National Park rises from flat prairie to an elevation of some 450 metres above the surrounding farmland to form part of the Manitoba escarpment. It covers 2,978 square kilometres (1,150 square miles) of diverse landscape. Besides the escarpment with its eastern deciduous forest of trembling aspen, white birch, ash, elm and bur oak, the park includes northern boreal forest of white and black spruce, jack pine, balsam fir and tamarack, and open grasslands and meadows. Lakes, beaver ponds, small marshy areas and streams abound. As you walk the trails note the understory of small trees such as nannyberry and mountain maple and vines of Virginia creeper and bittersweet.

Riding Mountain's varied elevations and plant life support an excellent variety of bird species. Thirty-two trails provide access to the different habitats in the park. Trail guides and pamphlets showing location and distance are available at the park gate and Interpretive Centre. These guides describe the many trails and habitats in the park.

The townsite of Wasagaming is a good spot to begin birding. Check the tall spruce for Yellow-rumped, Black-throated Green and Blackburnian

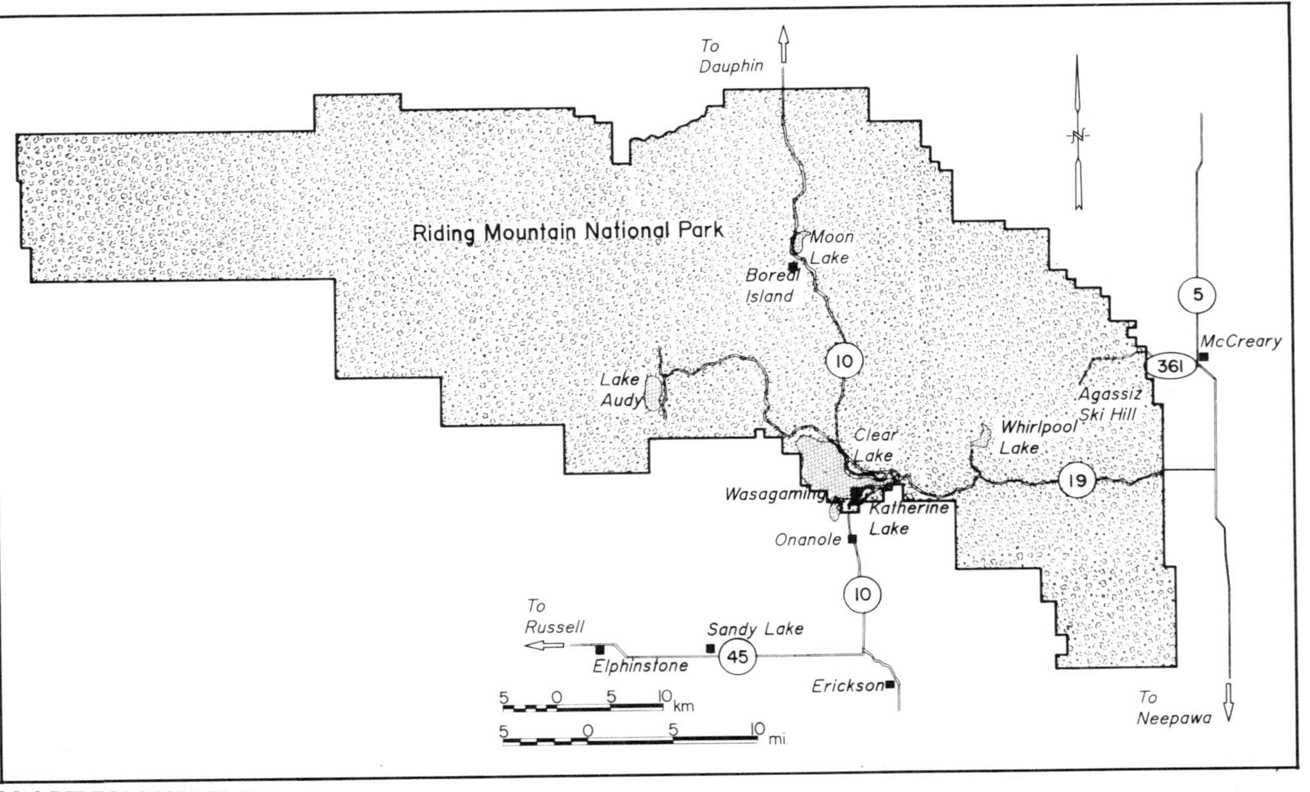

M13 RIDING MOUNTAIN NATIONAL PARK

Warblers and nesting Merlins. Watch for Gray Jay and Boreal Chickadee, Golden- and Ruby-crowned Kinglets, and crossbills.

Travel 9 km east of Wasagaming via PTH 19 to the Lake Katherine turnoff. At this point listen for Connecticut and Mourning Warblers. On the road into Lake Katherine watch for Solitary Vireo, Nashville Warbler and Ovenbird. Loon's Island trail (2.4 km) begins at the parking lot on the north shore of Lake Katherine and passes Loon's Island where a pair of nesting Common Loons may be observed. Keep an eye out for Pileated Woodpecker which frequents the area.

Return to PTH 19 and travel east through the boreal forest to Whirlpool Lake turnoff (approx. 7.5 km), making several stops along the way. Yellow-bellied Flycatchers have been heard in boggy areas off the road. Check pockets of unburned conifers for Spruce Grouse. Most sightings in the park of Manitoba's provincial bird, the Great Gray Owl, occur along this road. In the spring of 1980 a major forest fire created burned areas along this route. These burned areas are conspicuous and are especially productive for Western Wood-Pewee, Eastern Bluebird and Lincoln's Sparrow. This area also offers the best opportunity for seeing Three-toed and Black-backed Woodpeckers. At Whirlpool River check the alder thickets for Alder Flycatcher and Northern Waterthrush. Similar habitat occurs at Swanson Creek. At the Whirlpool Lake sign, turn left and drive north to the lake (approx. 3 km). A quick scan of the water may reveal Ring-necked Duck and Common Goldeneye. Winter Wrens have been heard to the east of the campground. A walk along Cowan Lake trail could produce Olive-sided Flycatcher and Western Wood-Pewee and is another opportunity for seeing Three-toed and Black-backed Woodpeckers.

Return to PTH 19 and continue towards the east gate, a distance of some 15 km. As you descend the escarpment through eastern deciduous forest the numbers and diversity of warblers are apparent. American Woodcock has been recorded in this area. Stop near the park warden station at the gate to check for Philadelphia Vireo and Scarlet Tanager. At the junction of PTH 19 and PTH 5 turn left and drive north to McCreary. At McCreary turn left onto the Agassiz Ski Hill Road (PR 361) and drive to the park boundary (approx. 5 km). This is an excellent road to check for several species not found elsewhere in the park. Explore the next 4.5 km within the park boundary for such species as Scarlet Tanager, Indigo Bunting and Rufous-sided Towhee. Chimney Swifts nest in the large tree snags in this area. Golden-winged Warbler is also a local breeder here.

Oak Ridge trail, 4.4 km inside the park boundary on the north side of the road, is a short loop of 3.0 km (or a longer loop of 6.4 km) and is another good place to listen for the buzzy notes of the Golden-winged Warbler.

Another interesting route to bird is along PTH 10. As you travel north through the park on this scenic highway you should make several stops for Red-breasted Nuthatch, Dark-eyed Junco and Purple Finch. If you wish to visit Lake Audy, with its bison enclosure, turn left at the turnoff and drive approximately 20 km on the Lake Audy Road. In the evening listen for Barred Owls along the first 4 to 5 km of the road. Bald Eagles are often seen near the lake and Sprague's Pipit is a possibility in the nearby grassland. By travelling north of the Lake Audy turnoff, on PTH 10, (approx. 15 km) you will reach the Boreal Island trailhead on the west side of the highway. Along the trail Cape May Warblers may be found. Moon Lake (1.6 km north along PTH 10) with some of the largest white spruce and balsam fir left in the park, can be a good area for Magnolia and Canada Warblers.

Riding Mountain contains many woodland ponds and small lakes where you easily find nesting Ring-necked Duck, Common Goldeneye and Bufflehead.

If you require a map or further information on the park, contact Riding Mountain National Park, Wasagaming, Manitoba R0J 2H0.

Northern Saw-whet Owl **Bob Horton**

Family of Burrowing Owls **John Murray**

Ferruginous Hawk Mike Conrad

Loggerhead Shrike Mike Conrad

SPECIALTIES OF THE REGION

RED-NECKED GREBE

Breeds in large sloughs and small lakes with emergent vegetation. Particularly good areas include Turtle Mountain Provincial Park and the region of small lakes north of PTH 16 extending into Riding Mountain National Park.

WESTERN GREBE

Nests in colonies on large lakes and marshes. Best viewing opportunities occur at the north end of Pelican Lake along PTH 23, Rock Lake and the Oak Lake/Plum Marshes.

CLARK'S GREBE

Recently found breeding at the north end of Pelican Lake along PTH 23 (Site 2). May occur elsewhere with Western Grebes.

AMERICAN WHITE PELICAN

Large numbers of non-breeders may be seen at Pelican Lake and Oak Lake/Plum Marshes through summer.

ROSS' GOOSE

Almost always seen with Snow Geese. Check flocks of Snow Geese feeding in stubble fields for this small goose. Watch for the rare blue phase.

WOOD DUCK

This beautiful but frequently overlooked bird can be found along most wooded streams, rivers, oxbows and even some beaver ponds. Good locations include Kitche Manitou and Marsh's Lake in Spruce Woods Provincial Park.

BALD EAGLE	In summer the best area to see this bird is around Lake Audy in Riding Mountain National Park. In late October and early November, Lake Wahtopanah, Oak Lake/Plum Marshes and Tri-Lakes area provide good viewing opportunities.
SWAINSON'S HAWK	This hawk is most common south and west of Brandon. When not soaring it is frequently seen on fence posts and utility poles. Several pairs nest annually in the immediate Brandon area.
FERRUGINOUS HAWK	Most of the breeding records are from the southwestern corner of the region. Recent nesting attempts have occurred north and east as far as Brandon. Check large open pastures from Pipestone to Lyleton (Site 5). This hawk may often be seen on the ground.
PRAIRIE FALCON	Check tops of hay bales and hay stacks in open country, especially late July through September. Better sites include the Oak Lake/Plum Marshes and Whitewater Lake areas.
GRAY PARTRIDGE	Widespread but primarily found in or near farmsteads, shelterbelts, edges of fields, roadsides (See Routes 1 and 2). In winter, coveys may also be found near feedlots.
SPRUCE GROUSE	Look for this elusive bird along PTH 19 through Riding Mountain National Park in pockets of unburned coniferous forest.

SHARP-TAILED GROUSE

Widespread throughout the region. Primarily found in or near brushy pastureland and prairie. Frequents gravel roadsides in winter. Good spots near Brandon are the Kemnay area, Chater area and pastureland to the southeast of Brandon (See Routes 1 and 2).

YELLOW RAIL

The best known location in the region is the Douglas Marsh. Listen for this rail along the road leading south from the village of Douglas, evenings and night (See Route 3). May be more widespread elsewhere in the region than records indicate.

AMERICAN AVOCET

Whitewater Lake is the best locality in the region for both nesting and staging (See Site 4). The east shoreline of Oak Lake can also be a good location. To the north of the Oak Lake Resort, 1.6 km north of the junction of PR 255 and PR 254, a large saline pond frequently harbors some of these birds.

UPLAND SANDPIPER

Most common in the southwest corner but occurs locally elsewhere. Near Brandon, the Shilo Plains provide good viewing opportunities. Follow any roads through the prairie west of Shilo (See Route 3). Check fence posts. The distinctive call can be heard from a distance.

MARBLED GODWIT

Check the large areas of mixed-grass prairie near Shilo (See Route 3). Other good spots are in the pastureland and hayland near Oak Lake/Plum Marshes. Follow PR 254 from the Oak Lake Resort to PTH 2. Large staging flocks occur by midsummer.

SNOWY OWL	Check fields, power poles, hay stacks, fence posts, in open areas, for this attractive winter visitor. Although it can appear almost anywhere, the Brandon airport, Alexander-Griswold Marshes and Oak Lake/Plum Marshes areas are good bets.
BURROWING OWL	The open pasture areas of Lyleton and Pierson provide the best possibilities of seeing this small owl. In July, family groups become conspicuous near their burrows. In recent years numbers have declined sharply.
GREAT GRAY OWL	Nesting birds have been found in recent years in burned areas along PTH 19 in Riding Mountain National Park. In winter a drive down any open road in this park may prove rewarding.
THREE-TOED and BLACK -BACKED WOODPECKERS	The best chances for encountering either woodpecker are along PTH 19 and PTH 10 in Riding Mountain National Park. Along PTH 19 check the burn areas. Listen for soft tapping. Check conifers for stripped bark. Both species are occasionally seen in winter outside of breeding area (Brandon, Rivers).
PILEATED WOODPECKER	Better sites include the Lake Katherine, Moon Lake and Clear Lake north shore trail areas in Riding Mountain National Park and Marsh's Lake in Spruce Woods Provincial Park. Occasional fall and winter sightings occur elsewhere.

WESTERN WOOD-PEWEE

The burnt-over areas along PTH 19 in Riding Mountain National Park offer the best opportunities for sightings. Elsewhere stands of dead trees caused by flooding or other factors may attract the species (See Route 4).

WILLOW FLYCATCHER

The willow swales in the Souris River region south of Melita and shrubby growth along the Chain Lakes provide the best opportunities to find this bird. Breeding was recently confirmed in the Melita area (Site 5).

SAY'S PHOEBE

The extreme southwest corner of the region, Lyleton and Pierson areas, is the best place to look (Site 5). However, breeding records have been reported east to Snowflake. Check old farm sites and abandoned buildings. Shy and retiring, it can be easily overlooked.

SEDGE WREN

The Douglas Marsh provides good habitat for this wren. Also check areas of unmown marsh meadows along PR 254 east of the Oak Lake Resort.

EASTERN AND MOUNTAIN BLUEBIRDS

Nest boxes on bluebird trails are readily used. A drive along PTH 5 through the Spruce Woods area provides good opportunities to see both species. The burn area along PTH 19 in Riding Mountain National Park is a good place to check for Eastern Bluebirds. Here natural cavities are used for nesting.

SPRAGUE'S PIPIT	Stops along PR 340 through the Shilo Plains or on adjacent roads should prove rewarding. Check any open pastureland from the Oak Lake area south and west to Lyleton. The distinctive overhead song reveals its presence.
YELLOW-THROATED VIREO	In Brandon this species occurs in Queen Elizabeth Park along the Assiniboine River. For another good location near Brandon refer to Route 2. Turtle Mountain Provincial Park is also recommended for this vireo.
GOLDEN-WINGED WARBLER	Occurs locally in Riding Mountain National Park in areas of bur oak with shrubby undergrowth. Regularly seen along Mt. Agassiz Ski Road west of McCreary. Also check the Oak Ridge trail.
CONNECTICUT WARBLER	Found in deciduous forest, mixed forest and spruce bogs. Good localities in Riding Mountain National Park include the Lake Katherine and Lake Audy roads off PTH 19 and PTH 10 respectively.
SCARLET TANAGER	Occurs regularly in the Brandon Hills Wildlife Management Area (See Route 2). The Kitche Manitou campground area in Spruce Woods Provincial Park is another good location. In Riding Mountain National Park, the mixed woods surrounding the Park Warden Station adjacent to the Mt. Agassiz Ski Road should be checked.

INDIGO BUNTING

Near Brandon, the municipal road through the Brandon Hills provides good sighting opportunities (See Route 2). PTH 5 through Spruce Woods Provincial Park, especially the Assiniboine River valley area, is worth checking. Any of the campground areas in Turtle Mountain Provincial Park may also prove rewarding.

LARK SPARROW

Check the dry, partially-wooded north slope of the Assiniboine River valley west of the junction of PR 459 and No. 1 Highway. Prime habitat of sandhill country with open woods is found along PTH 5 and PR 351 and adjacent roads through the Spruce Woods area.

LARK BUNTING

The extreme southwestern part of the region, Lyleton-Pierson area, provides the best viewing opportunities. Large pastures south of Pierson are good places to look for this bunting (Site 5). Annual numbers vary considerably.

BAIRD'S AND GRASSHOPPER SPARROWS

Near Brandon, listen for these sparrows in open prairie near Shilo, particularly along roads adjacent to PR 340. Elsewhere, large pastures, especially in the Lyleton-Pierson area, are worth checking (Site 5). Both species may occur in grain fields and hay fields.

LE CONTE'S and SHARP-TAILED SPARROWS

To locate these birds, stop and listen along the road south of the village of Douglas through the Douglas Marsh (See Route 3). Also check grassy areas around potholes along PR 262 south of Minnedosa. The marshy area just north of the Oak Lake Resort marina and another marshy area 1.6 km east of the Oak Lake Resort, both on PR 254, are good spots to check.

SMITH'S LONGSPUR

The open pasture and haylands north of PTH 2 between Pipestone and Oak Lake are good places to find Smith's Longspurs, especially in fall. Generally they appear in small flocks and their calls are heard first.

CHESTNUT-COLLARED LONGSPUR

The pasturelands of Shilo Plains offer good viewing. From the junction of PR 457 and the Waggle Springs road travel south to the Assiniboine River, checking pastureland along the way. Also see Route 4.

That's the wise thrush, he sings each song twice over,
Lest you should think he never could recapture
The first fine careless rapture!

—*Robert Browning*

NOTES

SPECIES LIST

Records covering a period of thirty years commencing with 1960 were considered in the preparation of this list of 294 species. The bar graphs show seasonal abundance. Accompanying notes give information on breeding habitat for species that nest in the region and favoured habitat during migration for other species. The breeding locations given are considered to be the best in the region.

Criteria used for supporting inclusion in the species lists were a photograph, a specimen, or a sighting by at least two competent birders.

Names are in accordance with the American Ornithologists' Union CHECKLIST OF NORTH AMERICAN BIRDS (6th edition, 1983), and the Supplements of 1985, 1987 and 1989.

LEGEND

▬	Abundant — can be observed on all visits in preferred habitat during the proper season, often in large numbers.
⫽⫽	Common — can be observed on majority of visits in preferred habitat during the proper season, numbers vary considerably.
—	Uncommon — is less frequently observed in preferred habitat, usually in low numbers.
• • • •	Rare — seldom observed but can be expected to occur annually.
O	Occasional — seven to twelve confirmed sightings since 1960.
O	Accidental — six or fewer confirmed sightings since 1960.
O	Isolated, out-of-season sightings.
●	Species breeds or has bred in the region.
?	Breeding suspected; verification needed.
*	Refer to Specialties of the Region.

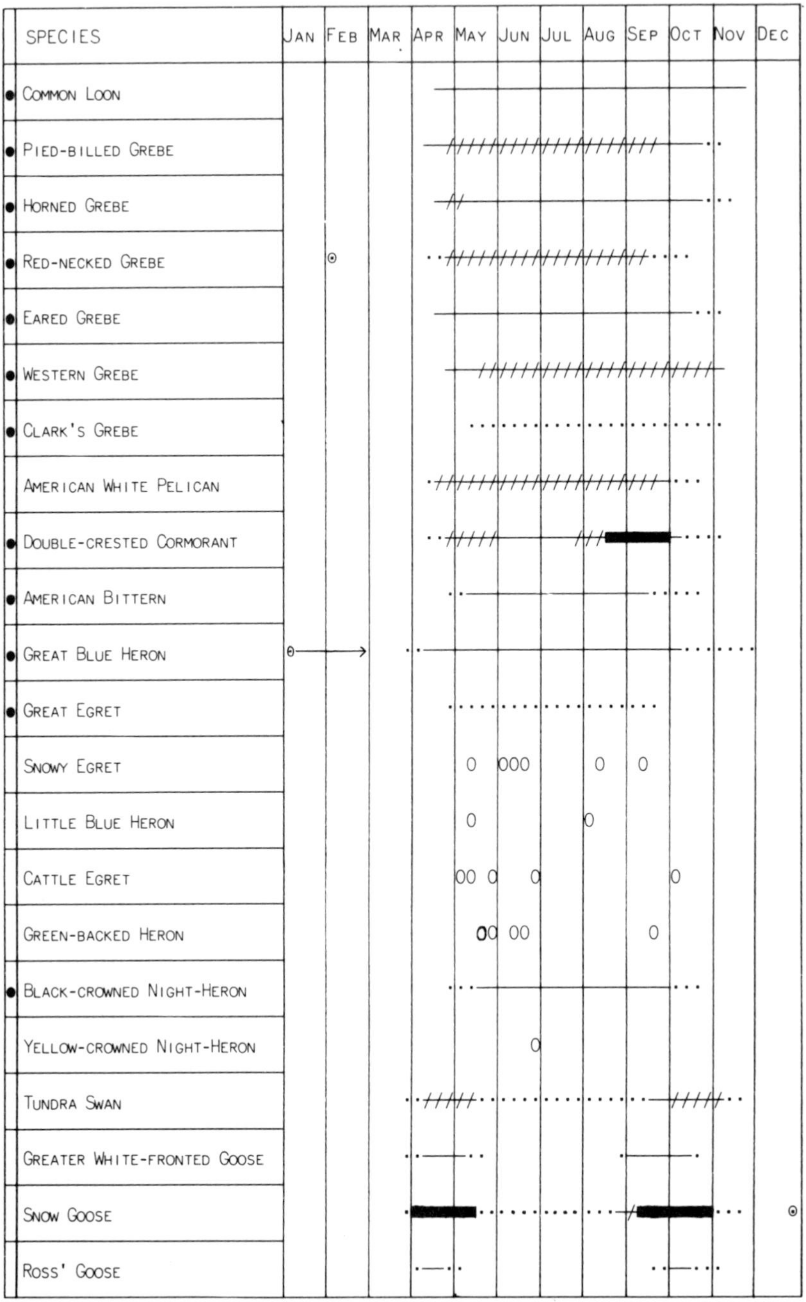

	SPECIES	JAN	FEB	MAR	APR	MAY	JUN	JUL	AUG	SEP	OCT	NOV	DEC
●	COMMON LOON												
●	PIED-BILLED GREBE												
●	HORNED GREBE												
●	RED-NECKED GREBE		⊙										
●	EARED GREBE												
●	WESTERN GREBE												
●	CLARK'S GREBE												
	AMERICAN WHITE PELICAN												
●	DOUBLE-CRESTED CORMORANT												
●	AMERICAN BITTERN												
●	GREAT BLUE HERON	⊖ →	→										
●	GREAT EGRET												
	SNOWY EGRET					0	000		0	0			
	LITTLE BLUE HERON					0			0				
	CATTLE EGRET					00 0	0				0		
	GREEN-BACKED HERON					00	00			0			
●	BLACK-CROWNED NIGHT-HERON												
	YELLOW-CROWNED NIGHT-HERON						0						
	TUNDRA SWAN												
	GREATER WHITE-FRONTED GOOSE												
	SNOW GOOSE												⊙
	ROSS' GOOSE												

COMMON LOON	Large and small lakes, nests in TMPP, SW area, RMNP, migrant elsewhere.
PIED-BILLED GREBE	Large marshes, sloughs, potholes (MPC).
HORNED GREBE	Sloughs, potholes, especially MPC.
*RED-NECKED GREBE	Small lakes, large sloughs, nests in TMPP, RMNP, sporadic elsewhere.
EARED GREBE	Colonial nester in large sloughs, marshes (Bone L., AGM, OL/PM).
*WESTERN GREBE	Colonial nester along lake edges (OL/PM, Tri-Lakes, Shoal L.).
*CLARK'S GREBE	Known to nest at Pelican L., possibly nests elsewhere.
*AMERICAN WHITE PELICAN	Summer resident at Tri-Lakes, OL/PM, Sandy L. area.
DOUBLE-CRESTED CORMORANT	Lakes, large marshes, nests in TMPP, Erickson-Rossburn area, uncommon summer resident elsewhere.
AMERICAN BITTERN	Marshes, sloughs, potholes (MPC, DM).
GREAT BLUE HERON	Rivers, marshes, lakeshores, nests locally in TMPP, RMNP, major river valleys.
GREAT EGRET	Rare visitant, one nest record near Pipestone.
SNOWY EGRET	Accidental at Pierson, Ninette, OL/PM, RMNP (L. Audy).
LITTLE BLUE HERON	Accidental at SWPP, Oak L.
CATTLE EGRET	Accidental at Pierson, Belleview, AGM, OL/PM, Brandon, Carberry.
GREEN-BACKED HERON	Accidental at Treesbank, Melita, TMPP, near RMNP.
BLACK-CROWNED NIGHT-HERON	Large sloughs, marshes (Glenboro Marsh, OL/PM, Erickson-Rossburn area).
YELLOW-CROWNED NIGHT HERON	Accidental near Mariapolis.
TUNDRA SWAN	Sloughs, flooded fields, large marshes; infrequent summer sightings.
GREATER WHITE-FRONTED GOOSE	Primarily in western part of region during migration (OL/PM, Whitewater L., Pierson areas).
SNOW GOOSE	Lakes, marshes, stubble fields; spectacular numbers can occur, particularly at Whitewater L. and OL/PM.
* ROSS' GOOSE	Primarily found in western part of region in association with Snow Geese.

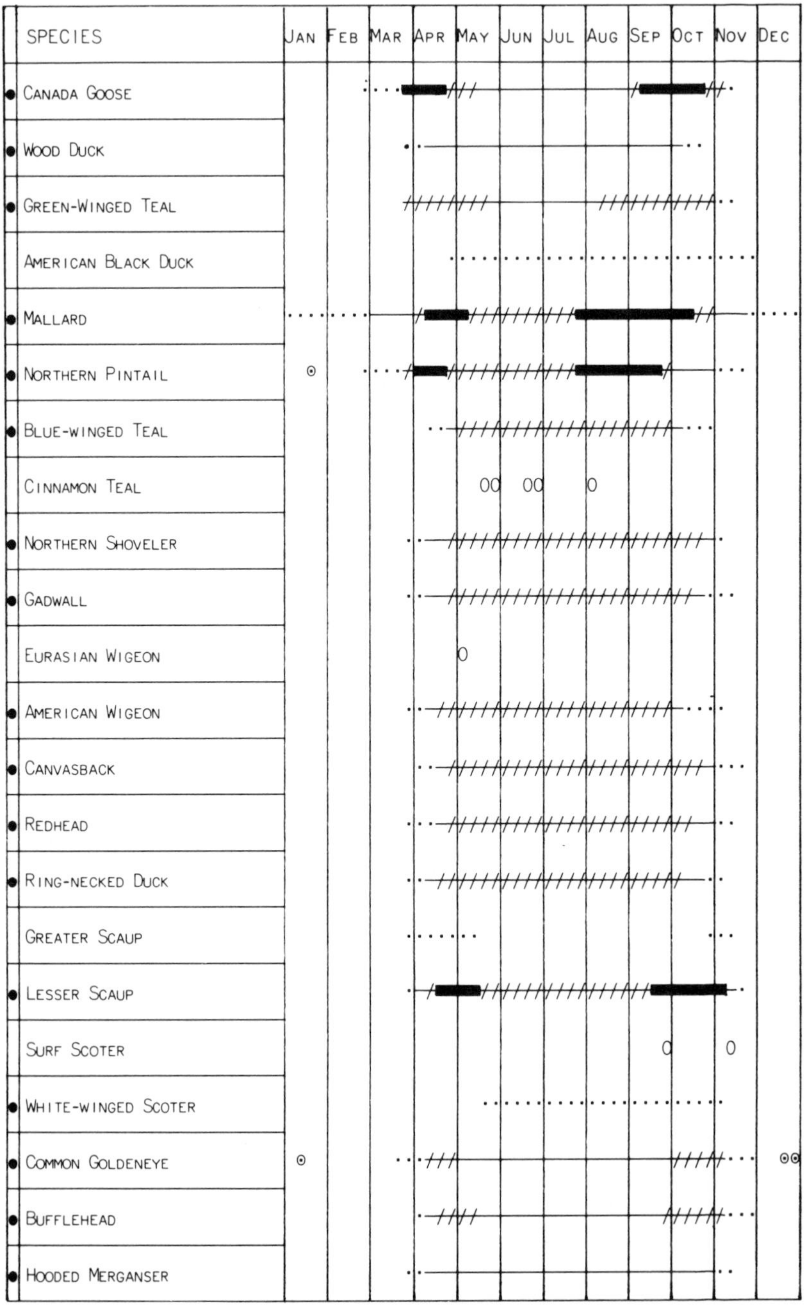

	SPECIES	JAN	FEB	MAR	APR	MAY	JUN	JUL	AUG	SEP	OCT	NOV	DEC
●	CANADA GOOSE												
●	WOOD DUCK												
●	GREEN-WINGED TEAL												
	AMERICAN BLACK DUCK												
●	MALLARD												
●	NORTHERN PINTAIL	⊙											
●	BLUE-WINGED TEAL												
	CINNAMON TEAL					00	00		0				
●	NORTHERN SHOVELER												
●	GADWALL												
	EURASIAN WIGEON					0							
●	AMERICAN WIGEON												
●	CANVASBACK												
●	REDHEAD												
●	RING-NECKED DUCK												
	GREATER SCAUP												
●	LESSER SCAUP												
	SURF SCOTER									0		0	
●	WHITE-WINGED SCOTER												
●	COMMON GOLDENEYE	⊙											⊙⊙
●	BUFFLEHEAD												
●	HOODED MERGANSER												

CANADA GOOSE	Large marshes, potholes, most evident in migration but larger race nests locally (OL/PM, MPC).
*WOOD DUCK	Wooded waterways, beaver ponds (Assiniboine R., Souris R., Pembina R.).
GREEN-WINGED TEAL	Prefers wooded ponds, large numbers stage at Whitewater L.
AMERICAN BLACK DUCK	Associates with Mallards, particularly at OL/PM, Whitewater L.
MALLARD	Widespread, potholes to large marshes.
NORTHERN PINTAIL	Widespread, potholes to large marshes.
BLUE-WINGED TEAL	Widespread, potholes, sloughs, conspicuous in late summer staging.
CINNAMON TEAL	Occasional near Brandon, OL/PM, Boissevain, Lauder.
NORTHERN SHOVELER	Widespread, potholes, sloughs, marshes; frequents sewage lagoons.
GADWALL	Widespread, potholes, sloughs, marshes, prefers large water bodies for staging (Whitewater L., OL/PM).
EURASIAN WIGEON	Accidental at Killarney.
AMERICAN WIGEON	Widespread, potholes, sloughs, marshes; less common than other dabblers.
CANVASBACK	Widespread, common nester in MPC, large numbers stage at OL/PM, Whitewater L.
REDHEAD	Widespread, potholes, sloughs, marshes, large numbers stage at OL/PM, Whitewater L.
RING-NECKED DUCK	Prefers woodland ponds (Erickson-Rossburn area, RMNP, TMPP).
GREATER SCAUP	Scarce migrant, associates with Lesser Scaup.
LESSER SCAUP	Widespread, sloughs, marshes, lakes; concentrations occur at L. Wahtopanah, OL/PM, Brandon Sewage Lagoon.
SURF SCOTER	Accidental at Oak L., L. Wahtopanah, Brandon Sewage Lagoon.
WHITE-WINGED SCOTER	Mainly seen in migration on large water bodies (OL/PM, L. Wahtopanah, Clear L.); recent breeding status uncertain.
COMMON GOLDENEYE	Woodland lakes, rivers, nests in Erickson-Rossburn area, TMPP, RMNP.
BUFFLEHEAD	Woodland lakes, beaver ponds, nests in TMPP, Tiger Hills, Erickson-Rossburn area, RMNP.
HOODED MERGANSER	Woodland lakes, rivers, local nester in TMPP, SWPP, RMNP, Little Saskatchewan R. valley.

	SPECIES	JAN	FEB	MAR	APR	MAY	JUN	JUL	AUG	SEP	OCT	NOV	DEC
●	COMMON MERGANSER												
	RED-BREASTED MERGANSER												
●	RUDDY DUCK												
●	TURKEY VULTURE												
●	OSPREY												
●	BALD EAGLE												
●	NORTHERN HARRIER												
●	SHARP-SHINNED HAWK												
●	COOPER'S HAWK												
●	NORTHERN GOSHAWK												
	RED-SHOULDERED HAWK												
●	BROAD-WINGED HAWK												
●	SWAINSON'S HAWK												
●	RED-TAILED HAWK												
●	FERRUGINOUS HAWK												
	ROUGH-LEGGED HAWK												
	GOLDEN EAGLE												
●	AMERICAN KESTREL												
●	MERLIN												
	PEREGRINE FALCON												
	GYRFALCON												
	PRAIRIE FALCON												

COMMON MERGANSER	Lakes, nests in RMNP, frequents lakes and rivers in migration.
RED-BREASTED MERGANSER	Prefers lakes in migration (Tri-Lakes, L. Wahtopanah, (OL/PM).
RUDDY DUCK	Widespread, potholes, sloughs, marshes, concentrations on large water bodies in migration.
TURKEY VULTURE	Summer resident in TMPP, SW area, RMNP, Assiniboine R. valley north of Virden.
OSPREY	Rivers, lakes, known to nest in TMPP, RMNP.
***BALD EAGLE**	Nests in RMNP, seen in migration along lakes, river valleys, large marshes, during October and November.
NORTHERN HARRIER	Widespread, marshes, large grassy meadows, hayfields.
SHARP-SHINNED HAWK	Known to nest in RMNP and TMPP, widespread in migration.
COOPER'S HAWK	Bluffs, woodlands.
NORTHERN GOSHAWK	Irregular winter visitor, nests in SW area, RMNP.
RED-SHOULDERED HAWK	Accidental at Shilo, Clearwater.
BROAD-WINGED HAWK	Nests in woodlands, migrates along river valleys.
***SWAINSON'S HAWK**	Widespread in open country.
RED-TAILED HAWK	Widespread, mixed woods to open country.
***FERRUGINOUS HAWK**	Local, prefers large open pastures.
ROUGH-LEGGED HAWK	Widespread migrant, numbers fluctuate yearly.
GOLDEN EAGLE	Rare spring and fall migrant.
AMERICAN KESTREL	Widespread, frequents powerlines, shelterbelts, bluffs.
MERLIN	Local nester, prefers spruce groves.
PEREGRINE FALCON	Prefers marshes, lakes (Whitewater L., OL/PM).
GYRFALCON	Check power poles, tops of spruce trees, in open country.
***PRAIRIE FALCON**	Open country, near Brandon see Route 4.

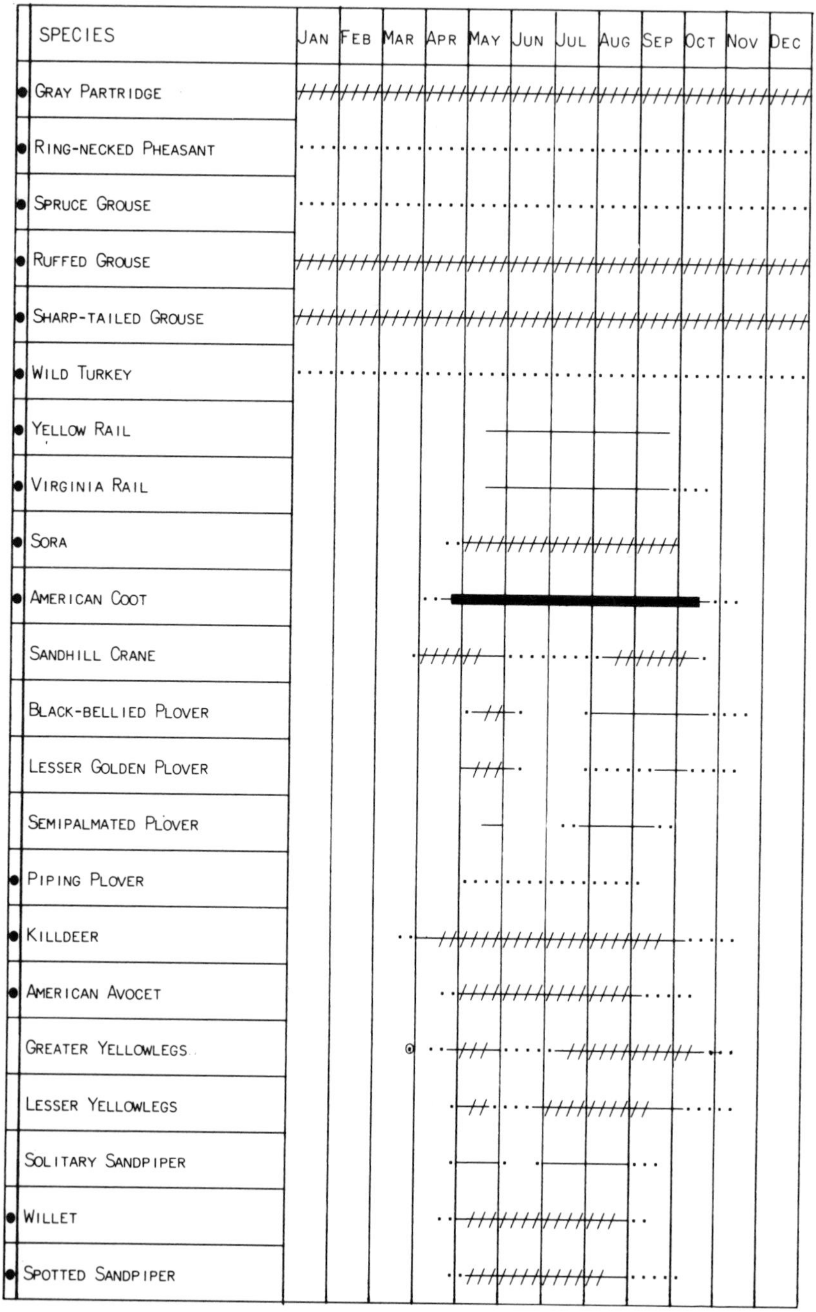

	SPECIES	JAN	FEB	MAR	APR	MAY	JUN	JUL	AUG	SEP	OCT	NOV	DEC
●	GRAY PARTRIDGE												
●	RING-NECKED PHEASANT												
●	SPRUCE GROUSE												
●	RUFFED GROUSE												
●	SHARP-TAILED GROUSE												
●	WILD TURKEY												
●	YELLOW RAIL												
●	VIRGINIA RAIL												
●	SORA												
●	AMERICAN COOT												
	SANDHILL CRANE												
	BLACK-BELLIED PLOVER												
	LESSER GOLDEN PLOVER												
	SEMIPALMATED PLOVER												
●	PIPING PLOVER												
●	KILLDEER												
●	AMERICAN AVOCET												
	GREATER YELLOWLEGS												
	LESSER YELLOWLEGS												
	SOLITARY SANDPIPER												
●	WILLET												
●	SPOTTED SANDPIPER												

***GRAY PARTRIDGE**	Widespread over agricultural land, numbers fluctuate.
RING-NECKED PHEASANT	Grassy ravines and roadsides, shelterbelts; sightings are probably released birds.
***SPRUCE GROUSE**	Occurs in RMNP.
RUFFED GROUSE	Wooded areas; highly cyclic.
***SHARP-TAILED GROUSE**	Widespread.
WILD TURKEY	Established in La Riviere area; recent introductions occur elsewhere.
***YELLOW RAIL**	Local in sedge and grassy marshes (DM, OL/PM).
VIRGINIA RAIL	Potholes, sloughs, large marshes, primarily in cattail (MPC, DM, OL/PM).
SORA	Widespread, potholes to large marshes.
AMERICAN COOT	Potholes, sloughs, marshes, large rafts in migration.
SANDHILL CRANE	Shallow wetlands, fields, large flocks in migration (Whitewater L., OL/PM).
BLACK-BELLIED PLOVER	Shorelines, mudflats, flooded fields.
LESSER GOLDEN-PLOVER	Shorelines, mudflats, flooded fields.
SEMIPALMATED PLOVER	Shorelines, mudflats.
PIPING PLOVER	Rare local nester along exposed shorelines (Whitewater L.), scarce migrant elsewhere.
KILLDEER	Widespread, roadsides, pastures, fields, shores.
***AMERICAN AVOCET**	Nests locally, saline ponds, mudflats.
GREATER YELLOWLEGS	Widespread, shorelines, mudflats, flooded fields.
LESSER YELLOWLEGS	Widespread, shorelines, mudflats, flooded fields.
SOLITARY SANDPIPER	Wooded ponds, roadside ditches, marsh edges.
WILLET	Nests in pasturelands, haylands, flocks occur in late summer.
SPOTTED SANDPIPER	Riverbanks, lakeshores, marsh edges.

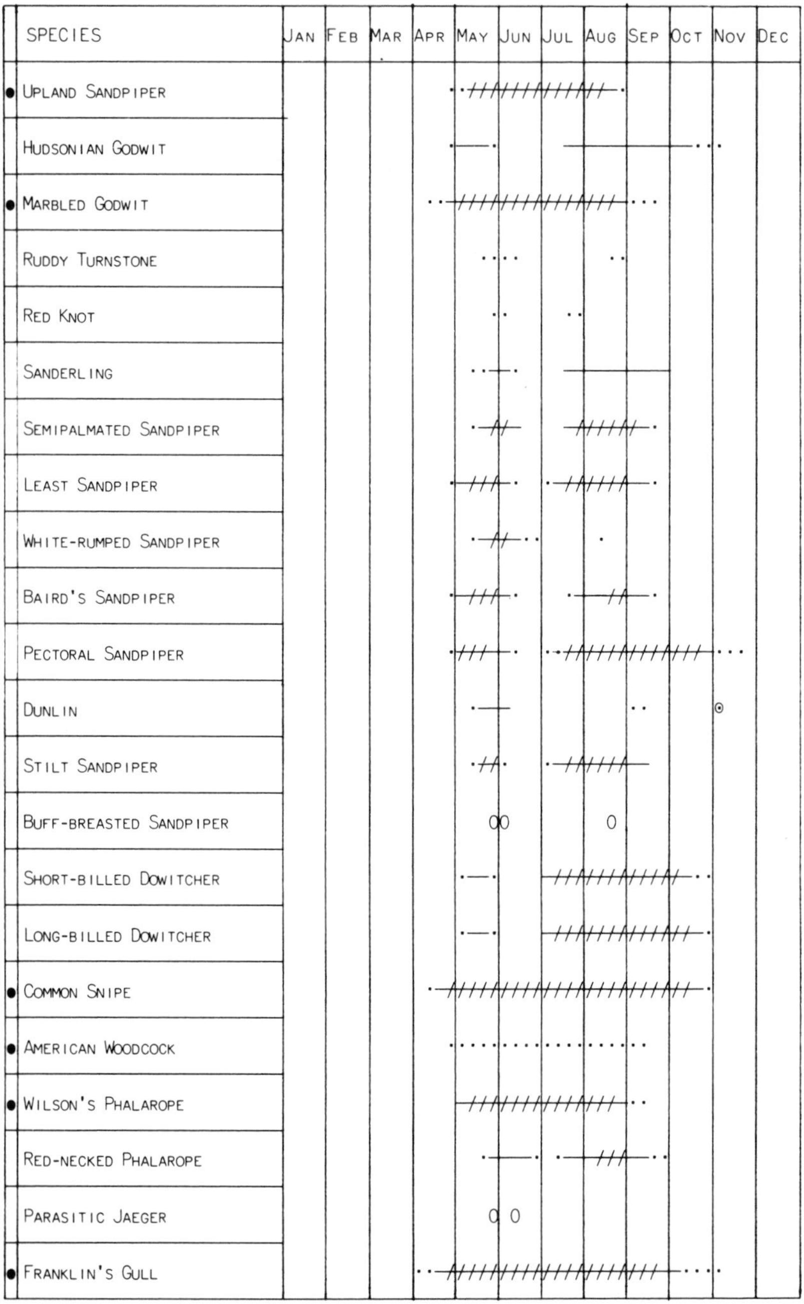

	SPECIES	JAN	FEB	MAR	APR	MAY	JUN	JUL	AUG	SEP	OCT	NOV	DEC
●	UPLAND SANDPIPER												
	HUDSONIAN GODWIT												
●	MARBLED GODWIT												
	RUDDY TURNSTONE												
	RED KNOT												
	SANDERLING												
	SEMIPALMATED SANDPIPER												
	LEAST SANDPIPER												
	WHITE-RUMPED SANDPIPER												
	BAIRD'S SANDPIPER												
	PECTORAL SANDPIPER												
	DUNLIN												
	STILT SANDPIPER												
	BUFF-BREASTED SANDPIPER												
	SHORT-BILLED DOWITCHER												
	LONG-BILLED DOWITCHER												
●	COMMON SNIPE												
●	AMERICAN WOODCOCK												
●	WILSON'S PHALAROPE												
	RED-NECKED PHALAROPE												
	PARASITIC JAEGER												
●	FRANKLIN'S GULL												

***UPLAND SANDPIPER**	Nests in pasturelands, haylands.
HUDSONIAN GODWIT	Vicinity of large water bodies (Whitewater L., OL/PM).
***MARBLED GODWIT**	Nests in pasturelands, haylands.
RUDDY TURNSTONE	Shorelines, mudflats of large water bodies (Whitewater L.).
RED KNOT	Shorelines, mudflats of large water bodies (Whitewater L., OL/PM).
SANDERLING	Shorelines (Whitewater L., OL/PM, Tri-Lakes).
SEMIPALMATED SANDPIPER	Shorelines, mudflats, flooded fields.
LEAST SANDPIPER	Shorelines, mudflats, flooded fields.
WHITE-RUMPED SANDPIPER	Shorelines, mudflats, flooded fields.
BAIRD'S SANDPIPER	Shorelines, mudflats, flooded fields; not always near water.
PECTORAL SANDPIPER	Shorelines, mudflats, flooded fields; often in mowed haylands near water.
DUNLIN	Shorelines, mudflats, flooded fields.
STILT SANDPIPER	Shorelines, mudflats, flooded fields.
BUFF-BREASTED SANDPIPER	Accidental at Oak Lake, Melita, Lyleton, Pierson WMA; check cultivated fields, mowed haylands, pastures.
SHORT-BILLED DOWITCHER	Shorelines, mudflats, flooded fields.
LONG-BILLED DOWITCHER	Shorelines, mudflats, flooded fields.
COMMON SNIPE	Widespread, damp grassy locations, marsh edges, willow swales.
AMERICAN WOODCOCK	Records from RMNP only.
WILSON'S PHALAROPE	Potholes, sloughs, marshes.
RED-NECKED PHALAROPE	Large bodies of open water (Brandon Sewage Lagoon, AGM, Whitewater L.).
PARASITIC JAEGER	Accidental at Waskada, RMNP.
FRANKLIN'S GULL	Local nesting colonies (Glenboro Marsh, OL/PM); frequently seen in cultivated fields.

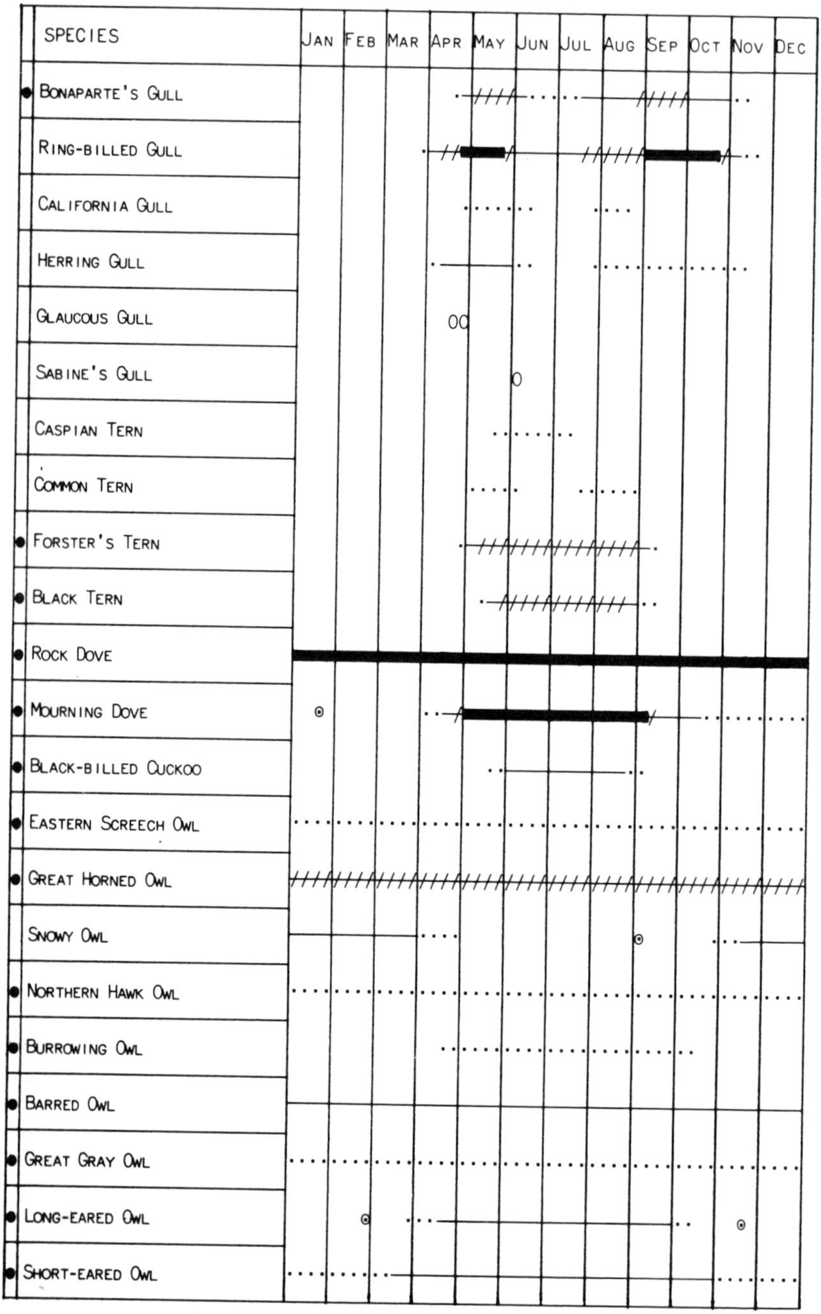

	SPECIES	JAN	FEB	MAR	APR	MAY	JUN	JUL	AUG	SEP	OCT	NOV	DEC
●	BONAPARTE'S GULL												
	RING-BILLED GULL												
	CALIFORNIA GULL												
	HERRING GULL												
	GLAUCOUS GULL												
	SABINE'S GULL												
	CASPIAN TERN												
	COMMON TERN												
●	FORSTER'S TERN												
●	BLACK TERN												
●	ROCK DOVE												
●	MOURNING DOVE												
●	BLACK-BILLED CUCKOO												
●	EASTERN SCREECH OWL												
●	GREAT HORNED OWL												
	SNOWY OWL												
●	NORTHERN HAWK OWL												
●	BURROWING OWL												
●	BARRED OWL												
●	GREAT GRAY OWL												
●	LONG-EARED OWL												
●	SHORT-EARED OWL												

BONAPARTE'S GULL	Nests in RMNP, elsewhere frequents large marshes and lakes (OL/PM, L. Wahtopanah, Whitewater L.).
RING-BILLED GULL	Lakes, marshes, cultivated fields, garbage dumps.
CALIFORNIA GULL	Records from Rivers, Brandon, Whitewater L., Tri-Lakes; often occurs with Ring-bills.
HERRING GULL	Lakes, marshes, garbage dumps.
GLAUCOUS GULL	Accidental at OL/PM, Brandon Sewage Lagoon, L. Wahtopanah.
SABINE'S GULL	Accidental at Clear L.
CASPIAN TERN	Large water bodies (Clear L., Tri-Lakes, Shoal L.).
COMMON TERN	Large water bodies (Clear L., Oak L., Tri-Lakes).
FORSTER'S TERN	Large marshes, lakes (OL/PM, Erickson-Rossburn area).
BLACK TERN	Potholes, sloughs, marshes.
ROCK DOVE	Urban areas, farmsteads, bridges.
MOURNING DOVE	Widespread, large concentrations occur in late summer.
BLACK-BILLED CUCKOO	Aspen bluffs, hedges, thick undergrowth; secretive.
EASTERN SCREECH-OWL	River-bottom woodlands; most sightings are in winter in conifers, farm buildings; primarily grey-phase birds.
GREAT HORNED OWL	Widespread; in winter prefers sheltered sunny locations.
***SNOWY OWL**	Open areas.
NORTHERN HAWK OWL	Coniferous and open mixed woods, nests in RMNP; may wander in winter; favours elevated perches.
***BURROWING OWL**	Open pastures.
BARRED OWL	Coniferous and mixed woods (RMNP, SW area); may wander in winter.
***GREAT GRAY OWL**	Spruce bogs, coniferous and mixed woods (RMNP).
LONG-EARED OWL	Nests in wooded areas of any size.
SHORT-EARED OWL	Open country, marshy areas; numbers fluctuate yearly.

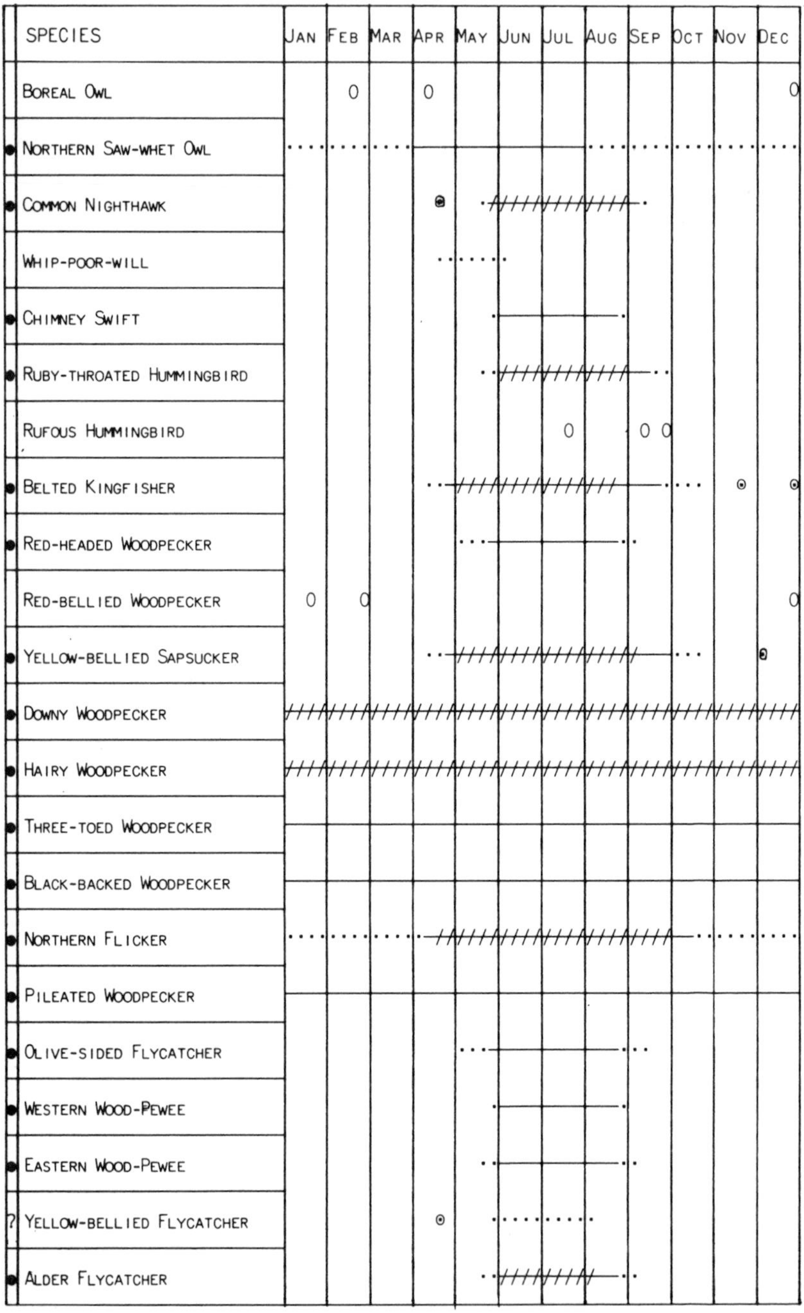

	SPECIES	JAN	FEB	MAR	APR	MAY	JUN	JUL	AUG	SEP	OCT	NOV	DEC
	BOREAL OWL												
●	NORTHERN SAW-WHET OWL												
●	COMMON NIGHTHAWK												
	WHIP-POOR-WILL												
●	CHIMNEY SWIFT												
●	RUBY-THROATED HUMMINGBIRD												
	RUFOUS HUMMINGBIRD												
●	BELTED KINGFISHER												
●	RED-HEADED WOODPECKER												
	RED-BELLIED WOODPECKER												
●	YELLOW-BELLIED SAPSUCKER												
●	DOWNY WOODPECKER												
●	HAIRY WOODPECKER												
●	THREE-TOED WOODPECKER												
●	BLACK-BACKED WOODPECKER												
●	NORTHERN FLICKER												
●	PILEATED WOODPECKER												
●	OLIVE-SIDED FLYCATCHER												
●	WESTERN WOOD-PEWEE												
●	EASTERN WOOD-PEWEE												
?	YELLOW-BELLIED FLYCATCHER												
●	ALDER FLYCATCHER												

BOREAL OWL	Accidental at Shoal L., Oak L., Lyleton.
NORTHERN SAW-WHET OWL	Mixed and deciduous woods (RMNP, SW area); may wander in winter.
COMMON NIGHTHAWK	Nests on flat gravelled surfaces (city rooftops); largest numbers in fall migration.
WHIP-POOR-WILL	Recorded in spring migration (Brandon, RMNP, near Reston).
CHIMNEY SWIFT	Local nester; chimneys (Brandon), large tree snags (RMNP - Mount Agassiz Ski Road).
RUBY-THROATED HUMMINGBIRD	Occurs in a variety of habitats, most conspicuous during August at flower gardens, feeders.
RUFOUS HUMMINGBIRD	Accidental at Lyleton, Brandon, OL/PM.
BELTED KINGFISHER	Rivers, creeks, lakes.
RED-HEADED WOODPECKER	Open woods, often containing large trees.
RED-BELLIED WOODPECKER	Accidental at Brandon, Souris, Cypress River.
YELLOW-BELLIED SAPSUCKER	Widespread, nests in a variety of wooded sites.
DOWNY WOODPECKER	Woodlands, bluffs; frequents feeders in winter.
HAIRY WOODPECKER	Woodlands, bluffs; frequents feeders in winter.
*THREE-TOED WOODPECKER	Resident in RMNP, possibly SW area.
*BLACK-BACKED WOODPECKER	Resident in RMNP and SW area.
NORTHERN FLICKER	Woodlands, bluffs, town parks, lawns.
*PILEATED WOODPECKER	Resident in RMNP and SW area in mature mixed woodlands.
OLIVE-SIDED FLYCATCHER	Mixed forests, generally near water; nests in RMNP and SW area.
*WESTERN WOOD-PEWEE	May be seen along PR 19 RMNP; rare elsewhere.
EASTERN WOOD-PEWEE	Mature river-bottom woods (Assiniboine R., Tri-Lakes), hardwood forests (RMNP escarpment).
YELLOW-BELLIED FLYCATCHER	Recorded at RMNP.
ALDER FLYCATCHER	Willow, alder swales, generally near water (DM, TMPP, RMNP).

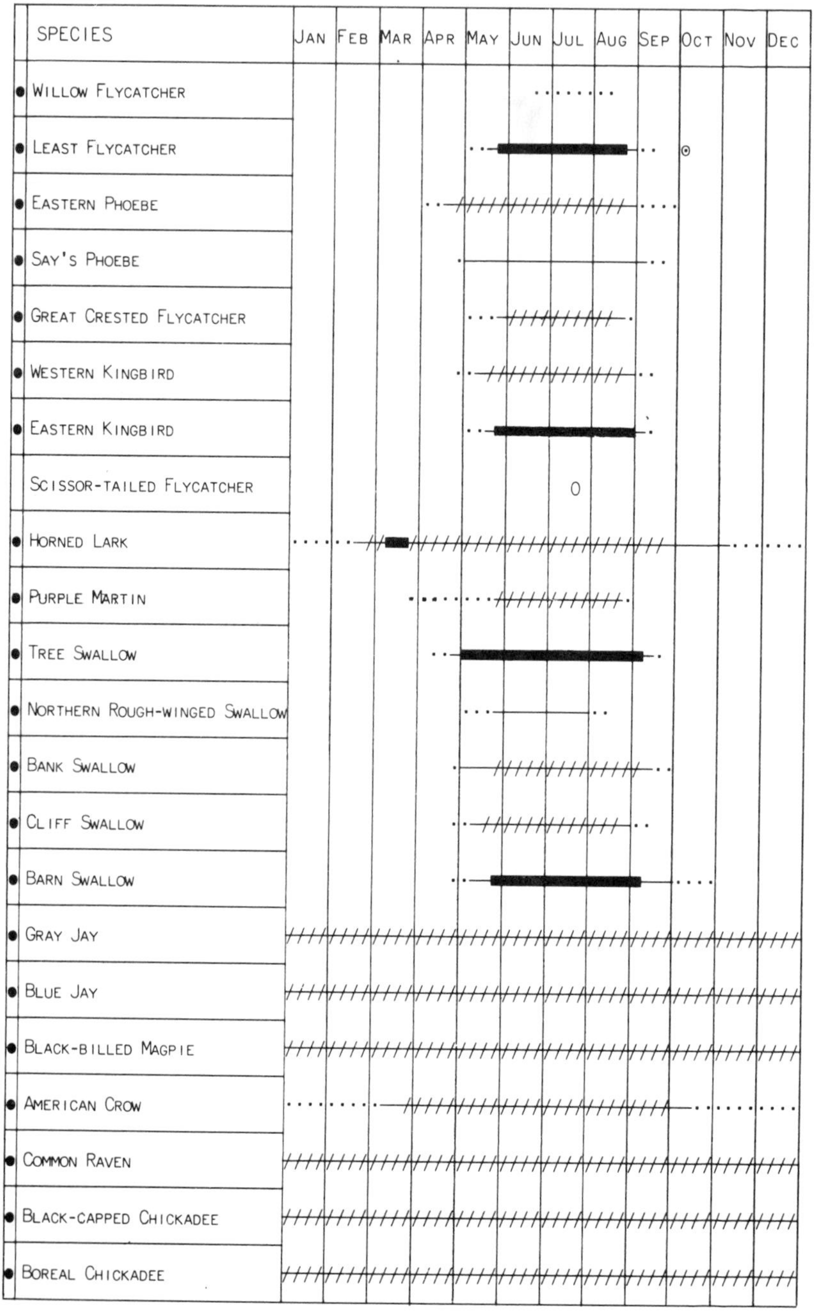

	SPECIES	JAN	FEB	MAR	APR	MAY	JUN	JUL	AUG	SEP	OCT	NOV	DEC
●	WILLOW FLYCATCHER												
●	LEAST FLYCATCHER										⊙		
●	EASTERN PHOEBE												
●	SAY'S PHOEBE												
●	GREAT CRESTED FLYCATCHER												
●	WESTERN KINGBIRD												
●	EASTERN KINGBIRD												
	SCISSOR-TAILED FLYCATCHER							O					
●	HORNED LARK												
●	PURPLE MARTIN												
●	TREE SWALLOW												
●	NORTHERN ROUGH-WINGED SWALLOW												
●	BANK SWALLOW												
●	CLIFF SWALLOW												
●	BARN SWALLOW												
●	GRAY JAY												
●	BLUE JAY												
●	BLACK-BILLED MAGPIE												
●	AMERICAN CROW												
●	COMMON RAVEN												
●	BLACK-CAPPED CHICKADEE												
●	BOREAL CHICKADEE												

*WILLOW FLYCATCHER	Willow clumps, shrubs, local in southwest corner.
LEAST FLYCATCHER	Widespread, woodlands, bluffs, towns.
EASTERN PHOEBE	Bridges, old buildings near creeks, rivers, lakes.
*SAY'S PHOEBE	Farmsteads, old buildings, mainly in southwest corner.
GREAT CRESTED FLYCATCHER	Widespread in deciduous woodlands.
WESTERN KINGBIRD	Shelterbelts around farm sites, towns; frequents fencelines.
EASTERN KINGBIRD	Edges of bluffs, roadside shrubs; often seen on fencelines, powerlines.
SCISSOR-TAILED FLYCATCHER	Accidental near Sidney.
HORNED LARK	Open fields, pastures; frequents roadsides in spring migration.
PURPLE MARTIN	Towns, villages, wherever Martin houses are present.
TREE SWALLOW	Nest boxes, tree cavities; large concentrations in late summer.
NORTHERN ROUGH-WINGED SWALLOW	Embankments near water (Souris R., Assiniboine R., Pelican L.).
BANK SWALLOW	Gravel pits, river banks, lakeshore embankments.
CLIFF SWALLOW	Bridges, buildings, occasionally steep river banks.
BARN SWALLOW	Nests in buildings and other man-made structures.
GRAY JAY	Local, coniferous and mixed woods (RMNP, SW area).
BLUE JAY	Wooded areas, urban and rural.
BLACK-BILLED MAGPIE	Widespread, especially in agricultural areas.
AMERICAN CROW	Widespread, large flocks in fall migration.
COMMON RAVEN	Resident at RMNP, SW area; fall or winter visitant elsewhere.
BLACK-CAPPED CHICKADEE	Widespread, woodlands and urban areas; frequents feeders in winter.
BOREAL CHICKADEE	Local, coniferous and mixed woods (RMNP, SW area); occasional elsewhere in winter.

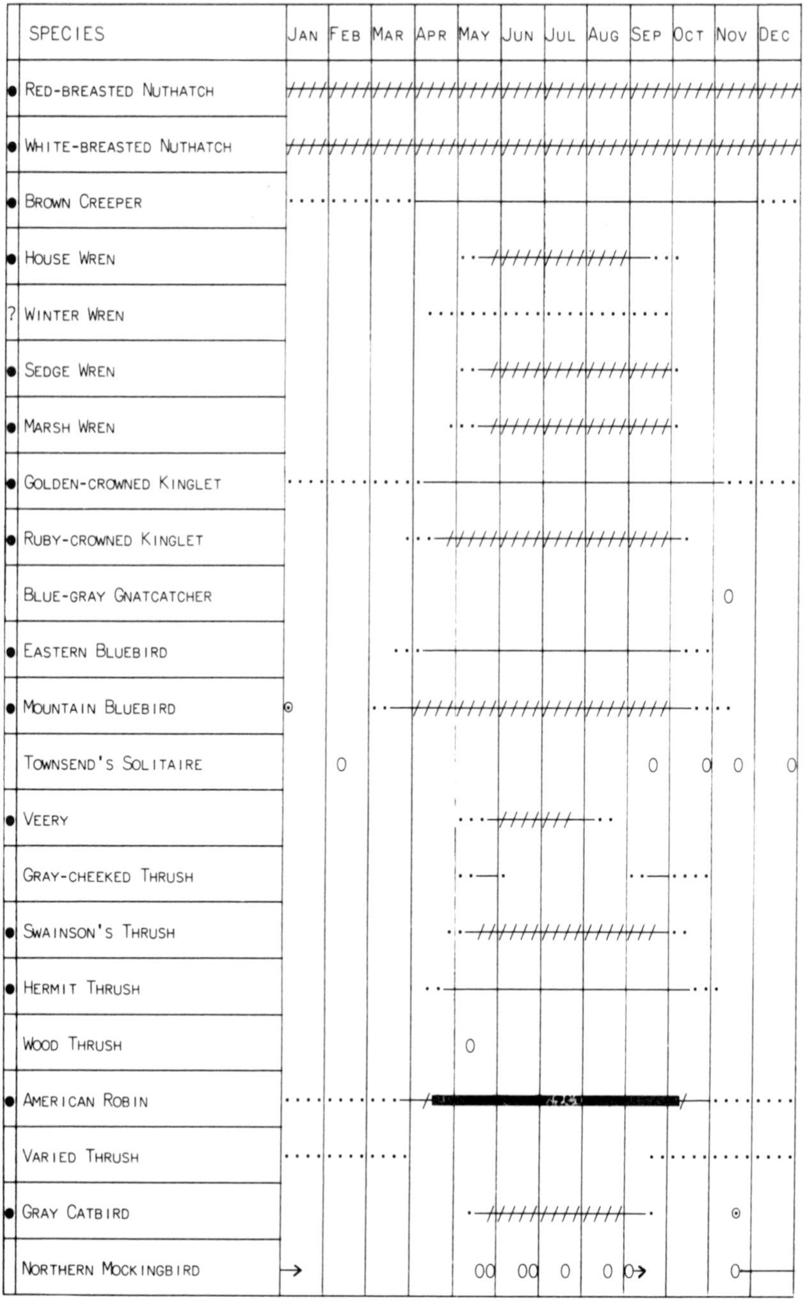

	SPECIES	JAN	FEB	MAR	APR	MAY	JUN	JUL	AUG	SEP	OCT	NOV	DEC
●	RED-BREASTED NUTHATCH												
●	WHITE-BREASTED NUTHATCH												
●	BROWN CREEPER												
●	HOUSE WREN												
?	WINTER WREN												
●	SEDGE WREN												
●	MARSH WREN												
●	GOLDEN-CROWNED KINGLET												
●	RUBY-CROWNED KINGLET												
	BLUE-GRAY GNATCATCHER											0	
●	EASTERN BLUEBIRD												
●	MOUNTAIN BLUEBIRD	⊙											
	TOWNSEND'S SOLITAIRE		0							0	0	0	0
●	VEERY												
	GRAY-CHEEKED THRUSH												
●	SWAINSON'S THRUSH												
●	HERMIT THRUSH												
	WOOD THRUSH					0							
●	AMERICAN ROBIN												
	VARIED THRUSH												
●	GRAY CATBIRD											⊙	
	NORTHERN MOCKINGBIRD	→				00	00	0	0	0→		0	

RED-BREASTED NUTHATCH	Coniferous and mixed woods (RMNP, SW area); frequents feeders in winter.
WHITE-BREASTED NUTHATCH	Widespread, woodlands, towns, villages; conspicuous at feeders in winter.
BROWN CREEPER	Coniferous and mixed forest, nests in RMNP.
HOUSE WREN	Widespread, bluffs, woodlands, towns, farmsites; uses nest boxes.
WINTER WREN	Mature spruce in moist locations; may nest in RMNP.
***SEDGE WREN**	Sedge meadows, grassy sloughs (DM, OL/PM).
MARSH WREN	Cattail marshes, sloughs, potholes (OL/PM, AGM).
GOLDEN-CROWNED KINGLET	Coniferous forest (RMNP, SW area).
RUBY-CROWNED KINGLET	Coniferous and mixed woods (RMNP, SW area).
BLUE-GRAY GNATCATCHER	Accidental at OL/PM.
***EASTERN BLUEBIRD**	Nest boxes, tree cavities; numbers increasing.
***MOUNTAIN BLUEBIRD**	Nest boxes, tree cavities; prefers pastureland with scattered trees.
TOWNSEND'S SOLITAIRE	Accidental at Brandon, Lyleton, SW area.
VEERY	Deciduous woods with thick undergrowth (Brandon Hills, Little Saskatchewan R. valley, RMNP).
GRAY-CHEEKED THRUSH	Shrub and bluff edges, lawns, in migration.
SWAINSON'S THRUSH	Mixed woods, nests in RMNP.
HERMIT THRUSH	Coniferous and mixed forest, nests in RMNP.
WOOD THRUSH	Accidental at Brandon.
AMERICAN ROBIN	Widespread, woodlands, farmsites, towns.
VARIED THRUSH	Observations from various localities, not of annual occurrence.
GRAY CATBIRD	Thick undergrowth, shrubbery.
NORTHERN MOCKINGBIRD	Observed or occasional at Pierson, OL/PM, Brandon, Shilo, RMNP, Broomhill, Tilston, Lyleton.

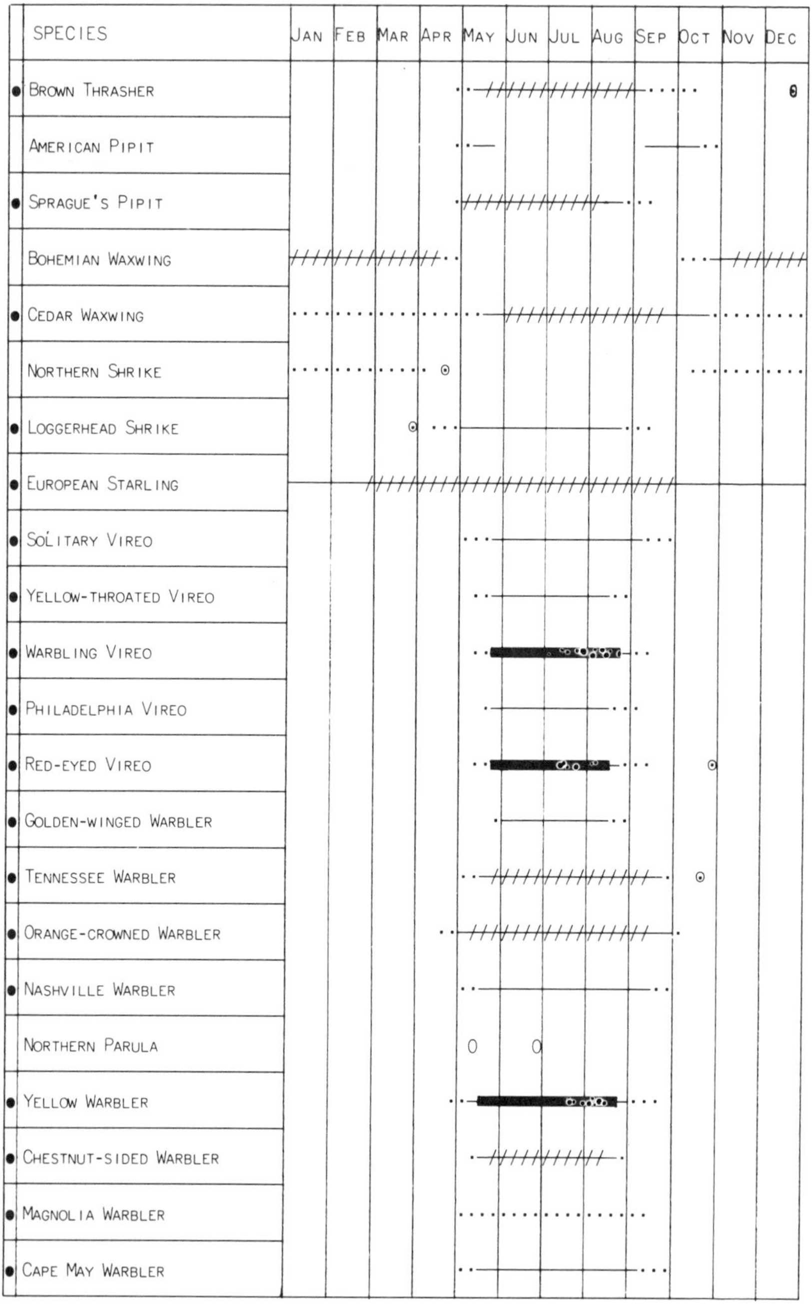

	Species	Jan	Feb	Mar	Apr	May	Jun	Jul	Aug	Sep	Oct	Nov	Dec
●	Brown Thrasher												
	American Pipit												
●	Sprague's Pipit												
	Bohemian Waxwing												
●	Cedar Waxwing												
	Northern Shrike												
●	Loggerhead Shrike												
●	European Starling												
●	Solitary Vireo												
●	Yellow-throated Vireo												
●	Warbling Vireo												
●	Philadelphia Vireo												
●	Red-eyed Vireo												
●	Golden-winged Warbler												
●	Tennessee Warbler												
●	Orange-crowned Warbler												
●	Nashville Warbler												
	Northern Parula					O	O						
●	Yellow Warbler												
●	Chestnut-sided Warbler												
●	Magnolia Warbler												
●	Cape May Warbler												

BROWN THRASHER	Thick undergrowth, shrubbery.
AMERICAN PIPIT	Open areas, generally near shorelines.
*SPRAGUE'S PIPIT	Open prairie, pastureland.
BOHEMIAN WAXWING	Widespread but erratic, frequents fruit trees, generally in large flocks.
CEDAR WAXWING	Parks, residential areas, edges of bluffs.
NORTHERN SHRIKE	Open areas; frequently perches on powerlines, fences, tree tops.
LOGGERHEAD SHRIKE	Shelterbelts, hedgerows, in open areas, especially around Lyleton-Pierson.
EUROPEAN STARLING	Widespread.
SOLITARY VIREO	Nests in RMNP, generally in mixed woods.
*YELLOW-THROATED VIREO	Prefers mature river-bottom woods.
WARBLING VIREO	Widespread in deciduous trees.
PHILADELPHIA VIREO	Prefers aspen woods, nests in RMNP.
RED-EYED VIREO	Deciduous and mixed woods, residential areas.
*GOLDEN-WINGED WARBLER	Nests locally in RMNP.
TENNESSEE WARBLER	Aspen and mixed woods, nests in RMNP and SW area, often large numbers in migration.
ORANGE-CROWNED WARBLER	Edges of mixed woods with thick understory, nests in RMNP and SW area.
NASHVILLE WARBLER	Mixed woods, nests in RMNP.
NORTHERN PARULA	Accidental at TMPP, Brandon, RMNP.
YELLOW WARBLER	Widespread in thick underbrush, hedges.
CHESTNUT-SIDED WARBLER	Second-growth deciduous and mixed woods, nests in TMPP, SW area, RMNP.
MAGNOLIA WARBLER	Mature mixed woods, RMNP (Moon L.).
CAPE MAY WARBLER	Mature coniferous woods, RMNP, SW area.

	SPECIES	JAN	FEB	MAR	APR	MAY	JUN	JUL	AUG	SEP	OCT	NOV	DEC
	BLACK-THROATED BLUE WARBLER					O		O		O			
●	YELLOW-RUMPED WARBLER												
●	BLACK-THROATED GREEN WARBLER												
●	BLACKBURNIAN WARBLER												
	PINE WARBLER					O			O				
?	PALM WARBLER												
●	BAY-BREASTED WARBLER												
	BLACKPOLL WARBLER												
●	BLACK-AND-WHITE WARBLER												
●	AMERICAN REDSTART												
●	OVENBIRD												
●	NORTHERN WATERTHRUSH												
●	CONNECTICUT WARBLER												
●	MOURNING WARBLER												
●	COMMON YELLOWTHROAT												
	WILSON'S WARBLER												
●	CANADA WARBLER												
	YELLOW-BREASTED CHAT						O O						
	SUMMER TANAGER				O		O						
●	SCARLET TANAGER												
	WESTERN TANAGER					O	O	O					
	NORTHERN CARDINAL					OO	O→						

BLACK-THROATED BLUE WARBLER	Accidental at Brandon, RMNP, Reston, Pierson, near Miniota.
YELLOW-RUMPED WARBLER	Widespread, coniferous and mixed woods (RMNP, TMPP, SW area).
BLACK-THROATED GREEN WARBLER	Mature mixed woods, RMNP (L. Katherine).
BLACKBURNIAN WARBLER	Coniferous and mixed woods, RMNP (Wasagaming), SW area.
PINE WARBLER	Accidental at Brandon, Pierson WMA.
PALM WARBLER	Widespread in migration.
BAY-BREASTED WARBLER	Coniferous woods, nests in RMNP.
BLACKPOLL WARBLER	Widespread in migration.
BLACK-AND-WHITE WARBLER	Moist deciduous woodlands.
AMERICAN REDSTART	Deciduous woodlands with dense undergrowth.
OVENBIRD	Deciduous and mixed woods.
NORTHERN WATERTHRUSH	Shrubby undergrowth near water.
***CONNECTICUT WARBLER**	Mixed woods, nests in RMNP (L. Katherine area).
MOURNING WARBLER	Deciduous woodlands with shrubby undergrowth (RMNP, SW area, TMPP).
COMMON YELLOWTHROAT	Shrubby areas near water.
WILSON'S WARBLER	May nest in RMNP.
CANADA WARBLER	Moist shrubbery in mixed woods, RMNP (Moon L.).
YELLOW-BREASTED CHAT	Accidental near Shilo and Bunclody.
SUMMER TANAGER	Accidental at Russell, Brandon.
***SCARLET TANAGER**	Deciduous and mixed woods (SW area, Brandon Hills, RMNP).
WESTERN TANAGER	Accidental at SW area, Shoal Lake, RMNP, Gladstone.
NORTHERN CARDINAL	Accidental at Brandon, OL/PM, TMPP, RMNP.

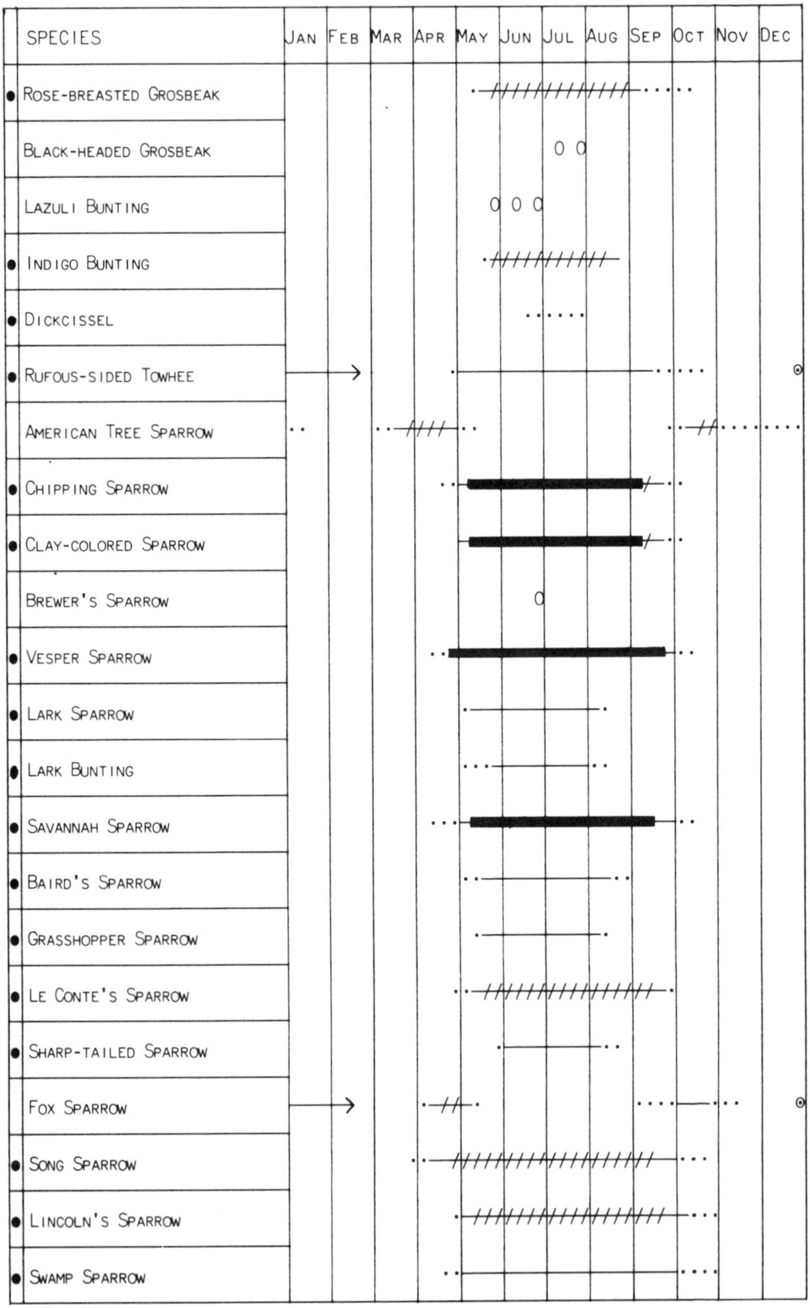

	SPECIES	JAN	FEB	MAR	APR	MAY	JUN	JUL	AUG	SEP	OCT	NOV	DEC
●	ROSE-BREASTED GROSBEAK												
	BLACK-HEADED GROSBEAK												
	LAZULI BUNTING												
●	INDIGO BUNTING												
●	DICKCISSEL												
●	RUFOUS-SIDED TOWHEE												
	AMERICAN TREE SPARROW												
●	CHIPPING SPARROW												
●	CLAY-COLORED SPARROW												
	BREWER'S SPARROW												
●	VESPER SPARROW												
●	LARK SPARROW												
●	LARK BUNTING												
●	SAVANNAH SPARROW												
●	BAIRD'S SPARROW												
●	GRASSHOPPER SPARROW												
●	LE CONTE'S SPARROW												
●	SHARP-TAILED SPARROW												
	FOX SPARROW												
●	SONG SPARROW												
●	LINCOLN'S SPARROW												
●	SWAMP SPARROW												

ROSE-BREASTED GROSBEAK	Mature deciduous woods, especially river-bottom.
BLACK-HEADED GROSBEAK	Accidental near Pierson.
LAZULI BUNTING	Accidental at RMNP, near Lyleton.
*INDIGO BUNTING	Local, edges of deciduous woods with thick undergrowth (Brandon Hills, SW area).
DICKCISSEL	Very sporadic, prefers alfalfa fields.
RUFOUS-SIDED TOWHEE	Prefers valley slopes where oak occurs.
AMERICAN TREE SPARROW	Seen in migration along roadside shrubbery, bluff edges.
CHIPPING SPARROW	Widespread, farmsteads, towns, open wooded areas.
CLAY-COLOURED SPARROW	Widespread, shrubby prairie, pastureland, bluff edges.
BREWER'S SPARROW	Accidental at DM.
VESPER SPARROW	Frequents shrubby prairie, pastureland, roadsides.
*LARK SPARROW	Prefers sandy areas with open woods.
*LARK BUNTING	Shrubby pastureland, primarily in the southwest corner, sporadic.
SAVANNAH SPARROW	Widespread, grasslands, shrubby pasture, fencelines.
*BAIRD'S SPARROW	Local, prefers grasslands (Shilo Plains, OL/PM, Lyleton).
*GRASSHOPPER SPARROW	Local, prefers grasslands (Shilo Plains, Lyleton-Pierson areas).
*LE CONTE'S SPARROW	Damp grassy meadows, grassy marsh edges (DM, OL/PM).
*SHARP-TAILED SPARROW	Usually wetter sites than Le Conte's Sparrow (DM, OL/PM).
FOX SPARROW	Shrubbery, hedges, bluffs.
SONG SPARROW	Prefers shrubby areas near water.
LINCOLN'S SPARROW	Local, nests in RMNP in burned area along PR 19.
SWAMP SPARROW	Wet brushy areas.

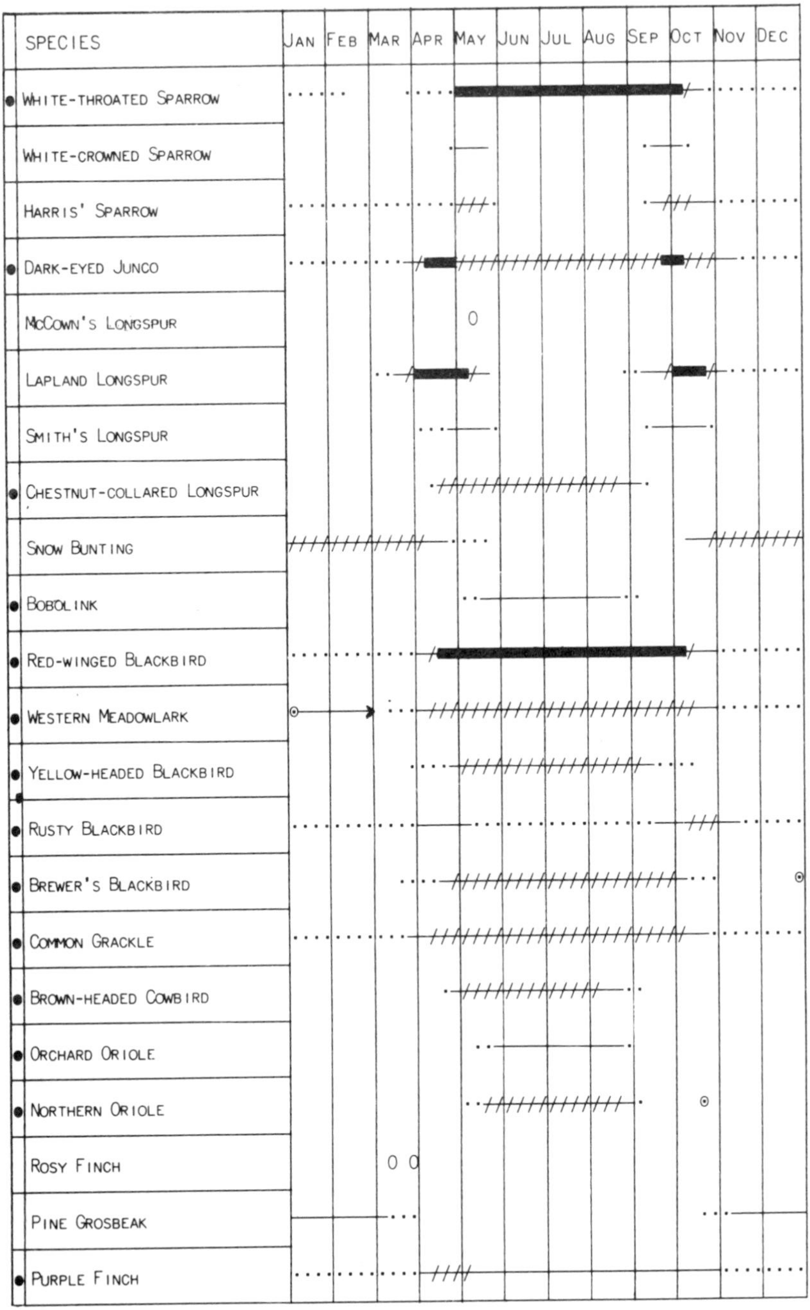

	SPECIES	JAN	FEB	MAR	APR	MAY	JUN	JUL	AUG	SEP	OCT	NOV	DEC
●	WHITE-THROATED SPARROW												
	WHITE-CROWNED SPARROW												
	HARRIS' SPARROW												
●	DARK-EYED JUNCO												
	McCOWN'S LONGSPUR					0							
	LAPLAND LONGSPUR												
	SMITH'S LONGSPUR												
●	CHESTNUT-COLLARED LONGSPUR												
	SNOW BUNTING												
●	BOBOLINK												
●	RED-WINGED BLACKBIRD												
●	WESTERN MEADOWLARK	⊙											
●	YELLOW-HEADED BLACKBIRD												
●	RUSTY BLACKBIRD												
●	BREWER'S BLACKBIRD												⊙
●	COMMON GRACKLE												
●	BROWN-HEADED COWBIRD												
●	ORCHARD ORIOLE												
●	NORTHERN ORIOLE										⊙		
	ROSY FINCH			0	0								
	PINE GROSBEAK												
●	PURPLE FINCH												

WHITE-THROATED SPARROW	Nests in RMNP, SW area; in migration, shrubbery, hedges, bluffs.
WHITE-CROWNED SPARROW	Shrubbery, hedges, bluffs, often with Harris' Sparrow.
HARRIS' SPARROW	Shrubbery, hedges, bluffs.
DARK-EYED JUNCO	Nests in RMNP, SW area; widespread in migration.
McCOWN'S LONGSPUR	Accidental near Lyleton.
LAPLAND LONGSPUR	Widespread over open country, often in large flocks.
***SMITH'S LONGSPUR**	Open pastures, fields, usually in small flocks.
***CHESTNUT-COLLARED LONGSPUR**	Local, prefers grazed pastures, short mixed-grass prairie (Shilo Plains, Lyleton-Pierson).
SNOW BUNTING	Generally in large flocks over open country, erratic in occurrence.
BOBOLINK	Hayfields, moist meadows, alfalfa.
RED-WINGED BLACKBIRD	Marshes, sloughs, potholes.
WESTERN MEADOWLARK	Grassy roadsides, pastureland, hayfields.
YELLOW-HEADED BLACKBIRD	Colonial, cattail marshes, sloughs, potholes.
RUSTY BLACKBIRD	Rare breeder, RMNP.
BREWER'S BLACKBIRD	Widespread in pastures, along fencelines, in open country.
COMMON GRACKLE	Widespread, farm sites, urban areas.
BROWN-HEADED COWBIRD	Widespread.
ORCHARD ORIOLE	Farm shelterbelts, towns, in southern part of region.
NORTHERN ORIOLE	Widespread, nests in tall deciduous trees, aspen bluffs.
ROSY FINCH	Accidental at Erickson, Russell.
PINE GROSBEAK	Irregular winter visitor in small flocks, prefers coniferous trees and ash.
PURPLE FINCH	Local nester in conifers.

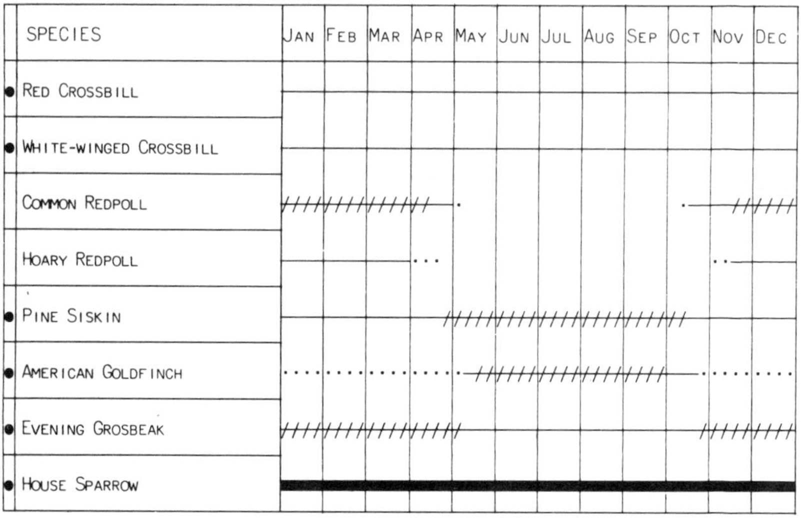

	SPECIES	JAN	FEB	MAR	APR	MAY	JUN	JUL	AUG	SEP	OCT	NOV	DEC
●	RED CROSSBILL												
●	WHITE-WINGED CROSSBILL												
	COMMON REDPOLL												
	HOARY REDPOLL												
●	PINE SISKIN												
●	AMERICAN GOLDFINCH												
●	EVENING GROSBEAK												
●	HOUSE SPARROW												

RED CROSSBILL	Erratic, generally near conifers.
WHITE-WINGED CROSSBILL	Erratic, generally near conifers.
COMMON REDPOLL	Frequents weedy fields, bird feeders, birch trees.
HOARY REDPOLL	Often with Common Redpolls in very small numbers.
PINE SISKIN	Irregular, prefers conifers, frequents bird feeders.
AMERICAN GOLDFINCH	Widespread.
EVENING GROSBEAK	Conifers, mixed woods, resident in SWPP, RMNP; numbers vary in winter.
HOUSE SPARROW	Widespread, urban areas, farmsteads.

HYPOTHETICAL LIST

Reports of the following species have been given consideration. However, they do not meet the criteria required for inclusion in the species list, the criteria being a photograph, a specimen, or a sighting by at least two competent birders.

- Pacific Loon
- Least Bittern
- Trumpeter Swan
- Brant
- Barnacle Goose
- Oldsquaw
- Black Scoter
- Barrow's Goldeneye
- Greater Prairie-Chicken
- Whooping Crane
- Whimbrel
- Long-billed Curlew
- Western Sandpiper
- Purple Sandpiper
- Pygmy Nuthatch
- Rock Wren
- Carolina Wren
- Phainopepla
- Cerulean Warbler
- Blue Grosbeak
- Field Sparrow

INDEX